Contents

Workbook introduction   **v**

1   NEBS Management Super Series 3 study links   v
2   S/NVQ links   vi
3   Workbook objectives   vi
4   Activity planner   viii

Session A   Understanding the market   **1**

1   Introduction   1
2   The market and competition   2
3   Product life-cycles   6
4   The marketing approach   9
5   **Summary**   18

Session B   The marketing mix   **19**

1   Introduction   19
2   The elements of the marketing mix   20
3   The people factor in the marketing mix   26
4   **Summary**   30

Session C   The right product at the right price   **31**

1   Introduction   31
2   The product   31
3   The product range   35
4   The right price   41
5   Product quality   44
6   **Summary**   49

Session D   The right place, the right time and the right way   **51**

1   Introduction   51
2   The right place   51
3   The right time   57
4   The right way: promotion   61
5   The right way: selling   62
6   **Summary**   68

Performance checks   **69**

1   Quick quiz   69
2   Workbook assessment   71
3   Work-based assignment   72

Reflect and review

73

1   Reflect and review   73
2   Action plan   75
3   Extensions   77
4   Answers to self-assessment questions   78
5   Answers to activities   80
6   Answers to the quick quiz   81
7   Certificate   82

NEBS
MANAGEMENT
DEVELOPMENT

SUPER SERIES

THIRD EDITION

Managing Activities

Marketing and Selling

Published for

& NEBS Management   *by*

Pergamon
Flexible
Learning

Pergamon Flexible Learning
An imprint of Butterworth-Heinemann
Linacre House, Jordan Hill, Oxford OX2 8DP
225 Wildwood Avenue, Woburn, MA 01801-2041
A division of Reed Educational and Professional Publishing Ltd

℞ A member of the Reed Elsevier plc group

OXFORD   AUCKLAND   BOSTON
JOHANNESBURG   MELBOURNE   NEW DELHI

First published 1986
Second edition 1991
Third edition 1997
Reprinted 1999, 2000

British Library Cataloguing in Publication Data
A catalogue record for this book is available from the British Library

ISBN 0 7506 3299 2

FOR EVERY TITLE THAT WE PUBLISH, BUTTERWORTH-HEINEMANN
WILL PAY FOR BTCV TO PLANT AND CARE FOR A TREE.

The views expressed in this work are those
of the authors and do not necessarily reflect
those of the National Examining Board for
Supervision and Management or of the publisher.

NEBS Management Project Manager: Diana Thomas
Author: Howard Senter
Editor: Petra Kopp
Series Editor: Diana Thomas
Based on previous material by: Howard Senter
Composition by Genesis Typesetting, Rochester, Kent
Printed and bound in Great Britain

Workbook introduction

Here are the workbook titles in each module which link with *Marketing and Selling*, should you wish to extend your study to other Super Series workbooks. There is a brief description of each workbook in the User Guide.

2 S/NVQ links

This workbook relates to the following elements:

A1.3   Make recommendations for improvements to work activities
D1.1   Gather required information

It will also help you develop the following Personal Competences:

- influencing others;
- focusing on results;
- searching for information.

3 Workbook objectives

'Marketing' has a kind of glamour. It makes us think of fashionable advertising agencies, and their high-flying 'creative teams', of costly and clever TV advertisements and large expense accounts.

Actually, this aspect of marketing is only the tip of the iceberg, and it is an area for specialists. Most managers, supervisors and team leaders will not take that route – they will work in the 'nuts and bolts' activities that keep the organization going from day to day.

There is another reason for steering away from the specialized aspects of marketing.

- Slack & Mallarky Transport was a family firm. When the old boss's university-trained son took over the reins, he borrowed heavily and spent £350,000 on 'relaunching the business in the market place'. There were new livery for the vehicles, uniforms for the drivers, new notepaper, an upgrade to the office and a trade advertising campaign. A sales manager was appointed at £36,000 a year plus car.

  Soon after, the firm went into severe financial crisis and was bought out cheaply by a competitor.

  The money spent on marketing did have an effect – sales initially increased but later fell back below what they had been before. Unfortunately, the new image was only skin-deep. The vehicles were smarter, but the service wasn't any more efficient. The office was full of new furniture, but information wasn't getting to customers any quicker. Worse, the cost of the 'marketing re-launch' was such that prices had to rise to cover it, leading to a loss of competitiveness that the new image was unable to redress.

The point is not that marketing campaigns are useless, but that there are limits on what they can achieve. Spending huge sums on advertising and publicity is no substitute for having the right product and an effective organization.

Success in the market depends primarily on offering customers a deal that is right – meaning as rapid, reliable, attractive, helpful and appropriate as possible for the price the customer is prepared to pay. And in particular, it depends on being able to provide at least as good a deal as your competitors do.

The product or service on offer is only part of the deal. In the long run, the back-up, service, style and behaviour of every part of the organization has an impact on the 'marketing mix' that it presents to its customers.

This is the marketing approach: making sure that everyone and everything in the organization is geared to meeting the needs of the market.

The implications should be clear. Every individual, every workteam, every manager, supervisor and team leader, whatever their specific function, does contribute in some way to market success or failure. You therefore have a responsibility to identify what you can do to support the marketing effort, and to lead your team in the right direction.

This workbook covers in some detail what it means to operate inside the market, what is meant by the marketing approach and what goes into the marketing mix. It focuses on the many ways in which supervisors' work can help or hinder their organizations' marketing efforts.

3.1 Objectives

When you have completed this workbook, you will be better able to:

- understand the meaning and importance of the market and the marketing approach;
- understand the marketing mix, and how an organization's resources are used to satisfy customers' needs;
- adopt the marketing approach and apply it to your everyday activities.

4 Activity planner

The following Activities require some planning so you may want to look at these now.

Activity 6 invites you to talk to other people in your organization to find a definition of the terms 'marketing' and the 'marketing approach'.

Activity 11 asks you to review what was done by your organization in terms of promotional and selling activity to market a new or recent product.

Activity 22 invites you to analyse your organization's range of products.

Activity 40 asks you to analyse the sales function in your organization.

Portfolio of evidence

Some or all of these Activities may provide the basis of evidence for your S/NVQ portfolio. All Portfolio Activities and the Work-based assignment are signposted with this icon.

The icon states the elements to which the Portfolio Activities and Work-based assignment relate.

The Work-based assignment involves reviewing what you and your team can do to provide your organization's customers with the right product, at the right price, the right place, the right time and in the right way. You may find it helpful to be thinking about these issues as you work through the sessions that follow.

Session A Understanding the market

Over the last 100 years whole industries have been swept away, and entirely new ones have come from nowhere. Caring for horses used to be one of the biggest service industries, with numerous stables in every town. Horse breeding was a large industry. On the light industrial side, tens of thousands of people earned their living by making harnesses and other equipment for horse-drawn vehicles. At the heavy end of the manufacturing spectrum, shipbuilding firms were thriving at ports everywhere in Britain. These were once major industries; today they have almost vanished.

On the other hand, even twenty-five years ago there was virtually no computer industry, no satellite communications and no video business.

Why have the old industries disappeared? They could draw on tremendous skills and expertise, and they had dedicated workers. The products they produced were often first-rate. The problem was simply that their customers didn't want those products anymore – there were other products on offer that they preferred.

This is a most important lesson. People are justifiably proud of their skills and expertise, even of the equipment they use. They tend to focus on the product and forget the customer. But making a top-quality stage coach when the customer wants an economical two-ton van is the road to ruin.

This workbook is about changing focus, about thinking about the market and the customer first and the product itself second. This may sound topsy-turvy, but meeting the customers' needs is what counts, and the product itself is just one part of that. Naturally this implies change; it may be painful at times, but organizations that don't change don't survive.

2 The market and competition

The word 'market' is used in many different contexts, for example:

- the Stock Market;
- the cattle market;
- the European Single Market;
- the export market;
- the money market;
- the commodities market.

2.1 What is the 'market'?

What do all these markets have in common?

Activity 1

8 mins

Think about your local open market – perhaps a fruit and vegetable market. Describe in about fifty words what goes on there.

_____

_____

_____

_____

_____

_____

_____

I would describe it like this:

- A number of different traders bring their goods and set them out on stalls. Then lots of potential customers come along and decide what they will buy, and from which trader they will buy it. The traders each try to sell their goods by offering the customer sharper pricing, or more attractive displays, or by shouting louder.

There are two things to notice about this description:

- the market forces the trader to face competition;
- the market presents the customer with choice.

However, the term 'market' in a general sense refers to a whole economic system which is conducted on this basis.

The market is simply the way in which the supply of goods and services, both nationally and internationally, is organized – though 'organized' is perhaps the wrong word to use about it. The market is not organized in the way that a factory or an office is. It is the net product of limitless numbers of buyers meeting limitless numbers of sellers, and hence of millions of individual purchasing decisions. The market is constantly changing and therefore very difficult to predict. It is almost impossible to control, except in very limited and specialized areas where there are few sellers and buyers.

But the market determines whether or not a particular product will succeed. This is the so-called 'law of supply and demand', and in this respect, the market is a mechanism for deciding, on a global scale, what goods and services will be produced and how much they can be sold for.

Every organization operates inside the market and, in some sense, lays its wares out on a stall in front of the buying public. For commercial organizations, success in the market is obviously crucial because it brings in the profits needed for survival. However, the 'market approach' is increasingly relevant to non-commercial organizations too – from hospitals, schools and government departments right down to voluntary bodies, social services departments and even prisons.

They all need to market themselves: they need funds, equipment, staff, 'clients', volunteer workers, donations and so on. And, just like industry and commerce, they have to compete to get them.

2.2 The product

People who work in the manufacturing industry will naturally think of the things they make as 'products'. These may be pipes or pickles, tanks or tintacks, but they are something physical that they can point to and say: 'That's our product.'

However, from the marketing standpoint, the term 'product' includes both physical objects of various kinds and what is usually thought of as services, such as insurance policies or TV rental packages.

Activity 2

List **five** 'products' offered by a typical high-street bank.

_____

_____

_____

> When a supermarket sells a piece of steak, what is the customer really buying? Not nourishment as such, because that could come from lentils, bread or tinned salmon. What the customer is really buying is a highly satisfying idea — the sizzle, not the steak, as marketing people often put it.

Financial institutions have many products (they do actually refer to them as 'products'). They include current accounts, deposit accounts, TESSAs, mortgages, loans, foreign exchange, bill payment services, insurance, savings plans, pensions schemes and so on.

These are what the banks try to 'sell' in their part of the market.

Throughout this workbook the word 'product' refers to whatever an organization has to offer to the market, whether that is goods, services or something else.

Something else? Some business experts believe that there is really only ever one product – satisfaction. That's over-simplifying things, but whatever kind of organization you work for, you should always remember that there is no future unless you can satisfy your customers' needs or desires.

2.3 Monopoly and competition

Imagine a world where there was only one source of a particular important product – say smoke detectors. This situation is known as a monopoly.

Everyone who wanted a smoke detector badly enough would have to go to that one supplier. The supplier wouldn't need to try very hard:

■ there'd be no need to bother with appearances: the business could be run from a dirty old shed;
■ convenience wouldn't matter much either: the firm could be located in Greenland;
■ publicity and promotion could be ignored – the customers would tell each other where to find the supplier;
■ service, packaging, quality and price would be of no importance.

In practice, monopolies are rather rare. In every area of activity that is capable of being profitable, there is always competition.

Activity 3

5 mins

Here are three different enterprises. For each one, say who its competitors might be and why.

The Tower of London

_____

_____

_____

Your local travel agent

_____

_____

_____

British Steel

_____

_____

_____

> 'The customer rarely buys what the business thinks it sells him. One reason for this, of course, is that nobody pays for a 'product'. What is paid for is satisfactions . . . Because the customer buys satisfactions, all goods and services compete intensively with goods and services that look quite different, seem to serve entirely different functions, are made, distributed, sold differently – but are alternative means for the customer to obtain satisfaction.'
>
> Peter Drucker,
> *Managing for Results*

The easiest of these to answer is the third one. British Steel competes with other steel-makers both in Britain and in various other countries. So British Steel competes in an international market for steel.

The first example, a famous tourist attraction, may have given you pause for thought. But tourist attractions do have to compete, even if many visitors specifically want to visit this particular place. In the long run, if the Tower of London were to become too expensive, or too shoddy, or if the staff were too unhelpful, it would lose out to other tourist attractions. So the Tower of London is in competition with all the other tourist sites in London.

To some extent the Tower also competes with other cities – Cambridge, Edinburgh, Paris or Rome – because it is part of London's general 'competitive pitch' for the international tourist market. And you can go a step further: the Tower also competes with other things that people could be spending their time and money doing, from watching TV to taking a river trip or going to the races.

The same applies to the local travel agent. Each travel agent has to compete with its business rivals, but it also has to compete with other products that families might spend their money on. A sum of £700 spent on a holiday could have been spent on new carpets, a hi-fi or dozens of other things.

So there are two points here:

- every organized enterprise faces competition;
- competition does not necessarily come just from the obvious business rivals.

Activity 4

5 mins

Now think about your own organization (or one that you know well).

a What are its main products?

_____

_____

_____

b Who are its main competitors?

_____

_____

_____

In thinking about these questions you have probably found that your organization does have competitors. You will see that, whatever part of the organization you work in, how you deal with that competition is a key issue for every employee in your organization.

Successful competition demands hard work, clear vision, skills and resources:

- the penalties of failure are decline, job losses, and eventually bankruptcy or take-over;
- the rewards of success are growth, expansion and opportunity.

3 Product life-cycles

You saw in the last section that the 'market' is all about the buying and selling of products – goods, services or whatever. But the market has a ruthless way with products, and even the most successful product has a limited life-cycle. The market is constantly changing, and unless the products also change, they will be left behind and forgotten.

Everyone knows the story of how in the nineteenth century lime juice was introduced to prevent scurvy. This unpleasant disease, which was once almost universal among sailors who went on long voyages, was purely the result of poor diet. What most people don't know is that lemon juice is actually far more effective at preventing scurvy, but that the British Navy switched to limes because they were cheaper — a market decision!

Organizations that want to survive longer than any of the particular products they offer, must do two things:

- modify existing products to ensure that they meet the requirements of today's market;
- introduce new products that will meet the needs of tomorrow's market.

In the business world this has produced some remarkable changes. One of the most spectacular transformations was that of the firm that makes Rose's Lime Juice. In the nineteenth century, it was a shipping company, and it supplied its sailors with lime juice to prevent scurvy. As the markets changed, the firm abandoned the shipping operation and concentrated on the lime-juice business!

Activity 5

3 mins

What new products (or services) has the organization you work for introduced in the last three years?

_____

_____

_____

It would be unusual if there weren't any new products – and it would be a danger sign. New products need to be developed to replace those that will soon go into decline. However, it may have occurred to you that another approach to this problem is to revamp existing products in various ways. The big car manufacturers are a good example of this. The Ford Fiesta, the Rover Metro and the Fiat Uno have been around for many years, but every two or three years the manufacturers carry out a significant upgrade and relaunch improved models on the market.

Successful commercial products typically pass through a four-stage life-cycle.

- Stage 1

Research, development, tooling and planning, production, promotion, advertising and launch on the market.

7

■ Stage 2

Rapid sales growth, competitive advantage and high profits.

■ Stage 3

Sales still good, but competition increasing and profitability declining (the market is 'mature'). This is the stage where upgrades are typically made, to try to prolong the product's useful life as a profit-maker.

■ Stage 4

Product outdated, fierce competition, price falling, sales and profits in decline (the market is 'saturated').

Of course, some products live longer than others, while many never get beyond Stage 2.

In graph form, the product life-cycle looks like this:

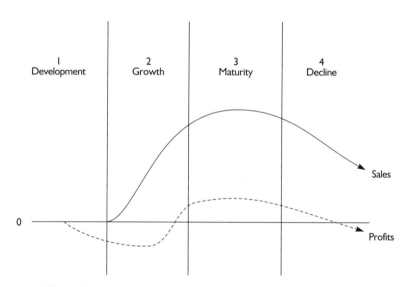

The product life cycle

Clearly, before the sales line starts dropping in Stage 3, new products must come into the picture, so that sales are kept stable overall.

The 80:20 rule (Pareto's Law) applies to products sold in the market: 80 per cent of the profit comes from 20 per cent of the products.

Because predicting the way the market will move in future is so difficult, most new products do not do well. The proportion that succeed in a big way is tiny (perhaps only 1 per cent). So most businesses try to keep up a steady flow of product innovation so that the chances of at least one product succeeding are reasonably high.

But even though it is difficult, the better we can predict the market, the less the risk of failure. That is an essential part of the marketing approach.

4 The marketing approach

For most people, the word 'marketing' conjures up the 'sharp end' activities such as planning advertising campaigns and getting the sales team mobilized.

4.1 A definition

This is indeed one part of marketing, but there is much more to it.

 Portfolio of evidence D1.1

Activity 6

 20 mins

This Activity may provide the basis of appropriate evidence for your S/NVQ portfolio. If you are intending to take this course of action, it might be better to write your answers on separate sheets of paper.

Talk to the people in your organization who are responsible for marketing, or its equivalent. Ask them how they would define 'marketing', then summarize your findings here:

_____

_____

Also ask them what they understand by 'the marketing approach', and summarize that similarly:

_____

_____

Finally, consider what this implies for you and your workteam. Note down any points that hadn't occurred to you before.

_____

_____

_____

There are several accepted definitions of marketing. A narrow one might be:

Marketing is about advertising and promoting the product to the customer.

In practice most marketing people do these things, and they also plan and interpret market research. Most modern organizations, however, would define marketing much more broadly, for example:

Marketing is about identifying and satisfying the needs of the customer.

This definition implies a range of **actions**:

1 **Market research:**

- finding out who the customers are;
- finding out what they need;
- finding out who else is trying to meet the need and at what price.

2 **Product development and distribution:**

- developing a product that meets the need;
- ensuring the product is made available at the right place, at the right time and in the right way.

3 **Promotion:**

- informing customers about the product (mainly advertising);
- encouraging them to choose it.

Another, simpler, way to put this is to say that marketing is about providing:

- the right product
- at the right price
- at the right place
- at the right time
- in the right way.

EXTENSION 1
If you would like to find out more about how the marketing approach works, and what happens to organizations that do not adopt it, I suggest you read D. Mercer's book, *Marketing*, which is listed as one of the extensions for this workbook.

Most organizations know that they have to engage in marketing. Many **do not** understand that success in an increasingly competitive marketplace depends on making sure that **everyone and everything** is focused on 'getting it right' for the market in every possible way.

This is what we mean by **the marketing approach**, as distinct from 'marketing'. It is the attitude that every aspect of the organization is relevant to market success and has to be managed in that light.

You could even call this a total marketing approach, because absolutely every aspect of the business is relevant to success or failure in the market.

4.2 Market research

Market research is about gaining greater knowledge and understanding of the market. It is a vitally important part of the marketing approach. But what knowledge do we need?

Activity 7

3 mins

EXTENSION 2
Market research is a way of getting reliable information about important issues. Any manager may find the basic skills useful from time to time. If you would like to go into the subject of market research in more depth and learn about some of the techniques involved, you might like to read *Do Your Own Market Research* by P.N. Hague and P. Jackson.

■ Ted and Lucy came into some money, and decided to give up their jobs to start a business making and selling radio-controlled models.

_____

What would you say were the three most important aspects of the market that they would need to research before making the decision to begin?

_____

_____

_____

It is most important to find out about the total size and money value of the market, and the nature and strength of the competition as they are at present:

■ how many people in the area are interested in these products;
■ how much they are likely to spend on them;
■ who the competitors are, what they do and where they are located.

Activity 8

3 mins

It is difficult for market research to predict the future, but try to suggest three things that researchers could investigate to help Ted and Lucy assess the future potential of the market for radio-controlled models.

_____

_____

_____

This activity may have been difficult for you if you have no previous knowledge of marketing, but perhaps you gave some thought to the sort of people who might be (or become) interested in expensive toys such as radio-controlled cars:

- what sort of people they are likely to be;
- how many such people there are;
- whether their numbers are likely to increase or decrease;
- what might be done to turn these potential customers into actual customers.

Market research is getting more sophisticated. Increasingly it is focusing on:

- lifestyles and attitudes rather than simply income and spending patterns;
- general economic changes that will influence spending patterns over a period of years.

The tasks of market research can be summed up as follows:

> **Market research needs to find out the present state of the market and how it is likely to change in the future.**

This applies to every kind of organization which operates in a market, whether its products are goods or services, whether it is large or small, and whether its market is local, national or international.

Market research is very big business – but it does not take decisions. That can be done only by managers, using the research figures, and perhaps helped by marketing specialists.

4.3 Product development and distribution

Every organization has to decide what attitude it will take towards its product and its customers.

Activity 9

3 mins

Which of these three attitudes is closest to that of your own organization?

Build a better mousetrap, and the world will beat a path to your door. ☐

Build a worse mousetrap, and spend a lot of money on advertising, and the world will beat a path to your door. ☐

Find out what sort of a mousetrap customers want, then produce it and tell them. ☐

The people who design and develop a new product are usually experts in their subject. Whether it is an insurance firm planning a new policy for people buying holiday homes abroad, or an electronics company designing a new type of car alarm, highly experienced and expert people will be involved.

However, left to themselves, the experts may come up with a product which does its job brilliantly but is too complex and expensive for the market. It may be 'over-engineered', in design terms. That is the 'Build a better mousetrap' attitude: a **product-led** operation.

Product-led organizations can find themselves deeply disappointed when their superb product fails to sell because it was what **they** wanted, but not what the **customer** wanted.

On the other hand, those organizations which don't care about product quality at all but expect the marketing people to 'hype' their way to success are also doomed to failure: a worse mousetrap will soon be seen for what it is.

The third attitude is more likely to be successful. The needs of the market override the needs of the product and its designers, so **market-led** organizations:

■ first study their market;
■ then give the development and production people a specification designed to meet the market's needs;
■ then get the product produced;
■ then market it in a positive and effective way.

Product distribution

The best promotional campaign can fail if the product isn't ready **and right** when it's needed. One of the worst disasters that can happen in marketing is for the customers to be ready and eager to take up a new product, only to find that some problem has held up delivery for days or even weeks.

■ A new range of six different cook-chill meals was due to hit the shops on 1 June. The advertising campaign was booked, with adverts on TV and in household and general interest magazines. Placards and special 'point of sale' materials were waiting at the retailers. A massive direct mail campaign was about to send millions of 'special offer' vouchers plopping onto consumers' doormats. 'Demonstrators' had been hired to promote the product in local stores.

Then, at the very last minute, disaster struck. The marketing people had assumed that a mixture of all six meals would be supplied to all the retail outlets, but no one had checked these arrangements with the production department. The factory had therefore gone for efficiency: it had made large runs of each individual meal and stored them in batches of 360 in special containers.

In supermarkets you will certainly have seen special promotional displays (often at the ends of aisles where they get most exposure). What you may not realize is that the selling power of these sites is so great that retailers can often **charge** suppliers for the privilege of placing their products there.

Someone was going to have to break all these up and repack them into mixed batches. The distribution company agreed to do this, but it was extremely expensive. It also took two days to complete. So, on 1 June, no products were available in the shops. Many retailers, unwilling to display empty promotional stands, cancelled their orders. Those that did persist, found that the shelf life of the meals was only three days instead of the expected five days. This caused all sorts of additional complications and ill-will.

If the distribution arrangements aren't right, even the most brilliant marketing campaign will be a waste of time and money.

4.4 Promotion

Three kinds of activity come under the general heading of 'promotion'.

■ **Advertising**

is about informing the market, to ensure that potential purchasers recognize and are attracted by the product. Generally this is intended to lay the ground for making a sale, rather than actually making it. Direct mail advertising is different: it tries to get customers to respond directly:

- by making a purchase by post or over the telephone;
- or by requesting further information (this is a means of introducing a sales person into the equation).

■ **Sales promotion**

covers many different techniques directed at potential customers and designed to create interest, generate enquiries and encourage sales. There is a huge variety of techniques, all working on the proposition that people find it difficult to resist anything that looks like a 'bargain'. They include:

- money off vouchers;
- competitions;
- gifts and other 'offers' that involve collecting and sending in labels, tokens etc.;
- 'buy five get the sixth free' offers.

■ **Selling**

is a direct approach by a human being and his or her persuasive skills. The days of the 'foot in the door' brush salesperson are more or less gone, but their telephone-based equivalents are alive and kicking. More importantly, there are many consumer products – especially higher-priced ones such as cars, insurance policies or kitchens – where customers expect a salesperson to be there to explain and negotiate. In the commercial and industrial field, selling is still a major area of activity. The salesperson or 'representative' plays a crucial role that is often quite complex.

Activity 10

10 mins

Talk to someone in your organization who regularly deals with supplier's reps. What do they expect from a rep, apart from the obvious 'sales pitch'?

_____

_____

_____

_____

_____

_____

To some extent the answer will depend on whether the rep is from an established supplier or from a new firm trying to 'break in'. In the latter case, the relationship is limited.

However, representatives from an established supplier are expected to do many things:

■   to keep the customer informed about technical and other developments;
■   to feed back comments, queries and complaints;
■   to help solve problems and to plan major developments;
■   to advise and assist the customer in getting the best from the product the representative is selling.

In return the representative gets regular opportunities to sell.

Session D covers these aspects of marketing in more detail. For now, Activity 11 asks you to make a review of the marketing techniques that your organization deploys.

Activity 11

20 mins

This Activity may provide the basis of appropriate evidence for your S/NVQ portfolio. If you are intending to take this course of action, it might be better to write your answers on separate sheets of paper.

Select one of your organization's new/recent products (those you identified in Activity 5).

First, find out about the period when it was first launched. What was done in terms of:

1   advertising

how much, where, when, and at what cost?

2   sales promotion

what techniques were used?

3   selling

where was the main selling activity directed; how did the representatives or telesales people go about it?

Second, get a view from those responsible on how effective each of these three parts of the marketing effort was.

Third, write up your ideas for improvements to the advertising, promotion and selling approach used.

If you are compiling an S/NVQ portfolio, it would be useful to add examples of advertisements, promotional materials and perhaps sales representatives' 'selling scripts' with comments attached.

Self-assessment 1

1   Fill in the blanks so that these statements make sense.

    a   The market forces traders to face _____ and presents customers with _____.

    b   The market is the net result of millions of individual _____ _____.

    c   The term _____ refers to whatever an organization offers to the market.

    d   Even the most successful product has a limited _____ _____.

    e   Market research is about gaining greater _____ and _____ of the market.

2   The marketing approach can be seen as providing:

    a   the right _____;
    b   at the right _____;
    c   at the right _____;
    d   at the right _____;
    e   in the right _____.

3   These letters make up the names of three important aspects of the marketing approach. What are they?

A	A	D	E	E	E	G	G
I	I	I	I	L	L	L	M
N	N	N	O	O	O	P	R
R	S	S	S	S	T	T	V

Answers to these questions can be found on page 78.

5 Summary

- The market is a system under which large numbers of traders offer goods or services for sale and large numbers of customers choose which to buy. The market is the net product of millions of individual purchasing decisions.

- Almost every organized enterprise faces competition; monopolies are rare.

- Competition does not necessarily come from the obvious business rivals.

- The goods, services or activities that an organization markets are known in general as its 'products'.

- All products have a limited life-cycle. Commercial organizations need to keep developing new products, to ensure their long-term survival.

- Marketing can be defined as 'The process of identifying and satisfying the needs of the customer'. It can also be seen as providing:

  - the right product;
  - at the right price;
  - at the right place;
  - at the right time;
  - in the right way.

- Every aspect of an organization is relevant to its success or failure in the market.

- Market research looks mainly at the existing market:

  - the number and location of the customers;
  - how much they have to spend;
  - who the competitors are.

- Market research also tries to predict how the market will be in the future; but this is difficult.

- 'Product-led' organizations start with their products, and then look for ways of marketing them.

- 'Market-led' organizations:

  - first study their market;
  - then specify a product that will meet the market's needs;
  - then produce the product;
  - then promote it effectively.

- The most successful organizations are market-led and adopt a 'total marketing approach'.

Session B The marketing mix

1 Introduction

'The marketing mix' is a jargon term, but the idea behind it is very significant, because every product on the market is different, even if the differences only seem small.

Take petrol, for example. All petrol of the same grade is basically the same regardless of whether it is sold by Shell, Texaco, BP or anyone else. Even the price does not vary greatly between different petrol retailers in the same locality. However, every petrol company presents its petrol to the public in a slightly different way. Some have extensive forecourt shops and other facilities, others simply have a kiosk. Some offer tokens, gifts and other promotional inducements, others don't. Some concentrate on big trunk-road sites, others go for smaller urban locations. Some put their staff in uniform, others don't. And overall, the style, decor, layout and advertising of the different companies are distinctly different.

All the details that distinguish an Elf station from a Q8 station, and from all the others, play a part in building up the overall 'package' that the company offers to its customers. Individually, the impact of the details may be quite small, but together they make up a distinctive **marketing mix**. (And, actually, the petrol is the least important part of the marketing mix for petrol companies: their marketing people regard the petrol station as the product, not the fuel sold there.)

These differences are crucial in enabling the rivals to compete. They cannot truthfully say things like 'Buy Octopus petrol because it makes your car go faster', but they can say 'Buy Octopus petrol because our service is better', or 'because our stations are cleaner and more modern' or 'because we share your particular lifestyle'.

2 The elements of the marketing mix

The marketing mix is the sum total of all the things that an organization does that have some impact on customers' attitudes to its product – the total 'offer' that an organization makes it to its market. Broadly, the elements are those we looked at briefly in Session A:

- the right product;
- at the right price;
- at the right place;
- at the right time
- in the right way.

An organization that gets all those elements right may not sweep the market, but it will be able to compete; one that doesn't won't even be in the running. This applies to non-commerical organizations as well as those whose main objective is to make profits.

2.1 Competing for customers

These days there are a lot of banks, and almost every town centre contains branches of up to a dozen different ones. They all offer a similar range of deposit accounts, current accounts, loans and mortgages, and they all have to compete with each other.

Activity 12

5 mins

Suppose you moved to a new town and decided to open a deposit account with a new bank. You have no particular preference, but you will need to visit the branch perhaps three or four times a month. There are six different banks in town from which you could choose.

List at least **five** factors that might influence your choice.

_____

_____

_____

_____

_____

_____

Price (in this context the rate of interest paid and charged) will obviously be a factor; most investors would try to find the best rate of interest in town.

But you would have to weigh price against other factors, such as **convenience**. If you have to visit the branch several times a month, you would probably prefer it to be located:

- in an easily accessible area;
- close to car parking facilities;
- close to the other facilities that you might need (such as shops, post office, library etc.).

Other convenience factors like **opening hours** might also count. Will the branch be open when you need it? Are enough staff on duty during busy times, so that you can avoid long waits? Do they offer other products that you might be interested in?

Then there is the **human factor** – the staff. Are they friendly, helpful, smart? Do they seem to have enough knowledge and expertise to talk sensibly about your needs?

And what about the general **style and decor** of the premises? Smart, scruffy, modern, old-fashioned, spacious, colourful, drab, warm, draughty, stuffy, noisy – these are all matters that have an impact on customers. Is the exterior clean? Is the window display neat and attractive?

Finally, there is the **image** of the bank created by its advertising. The banks spend large sums of money on informing the public about the products they offer, but their aim is also to build a particular image, which may be caring, efficient, business-like, hi-tech, relaxed and friendly, and so on. Like the decor and window displays of their local branches, these are not necessarily factors of which we are conscious when we make buying decisions, but subconsciously they do affect us.

> Some banks are former building societies, and a knowledge of this may also play a part in forming the image that customers have of them.

There is many a customer who can say 'No, I don't fancy that place', without being able to say exactly why. In reality, the customer's attitude is formed by the sum total of all the elements in the marketing mix, some of which are not immediately obvious, such as 'style'.

- CDT Sensors makes digital analysers – specialized machines for testing the circuitry of micro-electronic equipment. It sells a small range of products and accessories to companies which make and repair such equipment. Its market is this narrow slice of a few thousand business users. It does not sell to the general public at all.

  The company advertises in trade magazines, exhibits at trade shows and has four sales representatives who constantly travel the country.

Activity 13

4 mins

List at least **five** things that would probably be important elements in the marketing mix of a firm like CDT Sensors.

_____

_____

_____

_____

_____

In this case you already know about two factors that will weigh heavily:

■ the products themselves with all their features and benefits;
■ the advertising, promotional and selling activities.

Other important elements in the mix will include:

■ price, including discount structure;
■ availability of stocks and delivery lead times;
■ service and technical back-up.

There might even be special factors such as the amount of training offered to customers in how to operate the machines. And, of course, the details of every aspect of the operation will count, perhaps subconsciously: the reps, their cars, the quality of the exhibition panels and descriptive literature offered and so on.

The mixture of all these different elements is what CDT Sensors sets out on its 'market stall' to try and win customers; and its particular mixture needs to be different in some way to what its competitors are offering, in order to give it a competitive edge.

In summary, the marketing mix has a number of important aspects:

■ everything that has an effect on the customer is part of it, and this is true whether those concerned are aware of it or not;
■ some factors weigh more heavily than others;
■ customers make conscious decisions about some factors, but others have a subconscious effect.

In general, the most important elements of the marketing mix are:

■ the product itself;
■ the price;
■ the promotional and selling activities;
■ availability;
■ service.

If you wanted to analyse the marketing mix in more depth, you could try splitting the main elements into sub-elements. For the product, for example, these might include:

■ design;
■ quality;
■ packaging and presentation;
■ features;
■ colour scheme.

and many others. Marketing specialists would need to find something – however small – that gives the product a distinctive character. Such a 'unique selling proposition' (USP) is essential in making the product stand out from its competitors and giving the sales teams a 'handle' to work with.

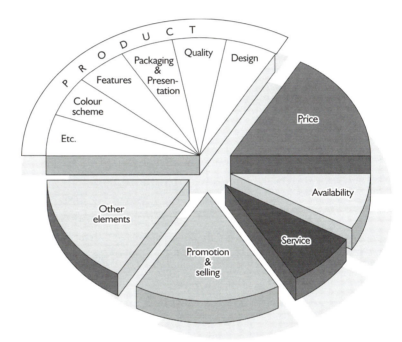

Typical elements in the marketing mix for a manufactured product

2.2 Maintaining customer satisfaction

All of the examples of elements in the marketing mix that we have considered so far are to do with the initial 'offer' – they are things that count when the customer is making the decision to buy. However, there are other elements in the mix which affect the **long-term** loyalty of the customer, and these are extremely important for an organization's survival in the market, even if they do not influence a new customer's **initial** decision.

Activity 14

3 mins

Long-term customer loyalty may be vital for the survival of both the bank and the electronics firm. List three factors which could influence customers to stay with, or to desert, their supplier:

_____

_____

_____

> Customers are loyal — but their loyalty is to their own interests. If suppliers fail to meet their needs, they can't expect to keep the customers.

The most important factor is likely to be the **performance** of the product. If a piece of equipment continually breaks down or underperforms, the customer is likely to become very disillusioned with the supplier. If the deposit account turns out to offer lower interest and less flexible terms than other products, including new ones entering the market, the bank's customer may close his or her account and switch to a competitor.

'Behind-the-scenes' factors also affect customer satisfaction, for example:

- the speed with which the supplier's staff tackle problems and queries;
- their attitude when doing so (which can vary from being eager to help to being downright hostile);
- the general efficiency of the organization (including details like spelling the customer's name right; sending post or deliveries to the right address; getting financial details correct first time; keeping a record of conversations, messages and appointments).

2.3 Dealing with dissatisfaction

Problems and complaints have a crucial influence on the long-term marketing position of any organization. Naturally, it is a good idea to produce a quality product with a minimum of faults and errors, but no one is perfect, and problems will occur in the most excellent of products. It is what happens after the customer has reported the problem that counts. Here is an example.

- Sheena rented a TV and video from Rapid Rentals. As part of the deal, it offered a refund if a repair took longer than forty-eight hours.

  One day, the TV broke down, and Sheena reported it. The following day, an engineer arrived and fixed it.

  Three days later, it broke down again. The engineer came after two days and fixed it.

  A week later, it broke down again. This time, the engineer did not come. After ten days, Sheena complained in writing to the managing director of Rapid

Rentals, and asked for the equipment to be removed and a refund given for the time it hadn't been working.

She received a very polite and apologetic letter from the MD, and the firm was prompt to remove the equipment and issue the refund. A few days later, however, Sheena received a letter from Rapid Rentals' accounts department, demanding a rental payment for equipment she no longer had. She returned this with a further letter to the MD. This time, the customer services manager wrote back apologising for the mix-up.

That should have been the end of the matter – except that within days Sheena received from the accounts department a new paying-in book for the following year!

Activity 15

3
mins

What would you say went wrong in the case of Sheena and the rental firm?

_____

_____

_____

_____

Clearly, the firm was badly organized: the left hand didn't know what the right hand was doing, and this always leads to problems. But organizational problems are always someone's responsibility:

■ **someone** should have noticed that this TV had broken down three times in rapid succession and done something about it;
■ **someone** should have made sure that when the rental contract was cancelled, the accounts department were informed.

Perhaps this organization should have employed a team of people specifically to ensure that service quality matched the promises the firm gave its customers!

Activity 16

No organization likes receiving complaints, but a number of leading companies now take the view that complaints can be positively beneficial in increasing customer loyalty. Try to suggest why this might be.

_____

_____

_____

_____

> **Bad news travels faster than good. Research has shown that when customers are satisfied, they tell around four other people. But when they are dissatisfied, they tell around ten.**

The logic goes like this:

- Some customers do not complain, they simply 'vote with their feet', i.e. they stop using the organization and go to a competitor next time.
- The long-term attitude of those who do complain depends on how well an organization deals with the complaint; customers whose problem is promptly, efficiently and pleasantly resolved are likely to have a **higher opinion** of the organization than they did before the problem arose; they become more loyal, not less.
- Complaints are an important source of feedback about how well a product is performing; if you listen carefully and take the necessary measures, you can improve your product in the future.

3 The people factor in the marketing mix

Every single aspect of an organization that a customer encounters will have some impact on that customer's attitude and therefore on his or her purchasing decisions.

Each aspect will either strengthen or weaken the organization's ability to succeed in the market. The effect of any one element in the marketing mix may be quite small, but even a very small 'minus point' may be enough to let in a competitor whose 'package' is marginally more attractive.

In this 'total' approach, it is obvious that people and the way they deal with customers will be particularly important. Every employee whose activities have an effect on the product or the customer contributes to market success or failure. In fact, the most successful organizations believe that **everyone on their payroll** is part of the marketing mix.

Activity 17

Here are four short descriptions of people working in quite different kinds of jobs. Think about each situation carefully, and then write down what you think about the impact on the organizations' marketing mix.

■ Sarah was credit control supervisor with a large firm of builders' merchants. She and her team spent at least three days every month chasing customers for payment of overdue invoices. 'Be hard as nails with them,' she told the others. 'Be as nasty as you like. Just get the money. Every £1 overdue is making us less competitive.'

What sort of effect is this likely to have on this firm's position in the market?

_____

_____

_____

_____

■ Sheila and Manjit were shelf-fillers in a supermarket. All they had to do was to re-stock shelves following detailed plans sent from head office. One day, a customer stopped and asked 'Can you tell me where abouts the sponge fingers are, please?' The two looked at each other. Manjit just shrugged and went on shelf-filling. Sheila said 'Sorry, dunno. You'll have to ask someone else.'

What do you think they should have done, and why?

_____

_____

_____

_____

■ Peter, a section manager in a factory producing packaging materials, received a phone call from Sally, one of the sales representatives. 'Peter, sorry to trouble you, but I'm with a customer and we need some information. Can you confirm a list of tensile strengths in various gauges for us?' Peter was not pleased: 'Look, young lady, I haven't got time for that sort of thing. I've got production targets to meet here. If you wanted that sort of information you should have thought about it beforehand. Goodbye.' Sally apologized to her customer as best she could: 'Sorry, we've got one or two awkward types back at the factory.'

What does this episode tell you about this company, and what effect will the incident have on its attempts to sell its products?

_____

_____

_____

_____

■ Danny was a service engineer for a water company and was allowed to take his van home at night. Almost every night he parked it in a spot which was very handy for him, but very inconvenient for some of his neighbours. There were numerous complaints.

Why should his employer be concerned about such a minor matter?

_____

_____

_____

_____

A marketing and customer service specialist would probably see it like this:

■ Certainly, as Sarah says, poor credit control affects profitability and hence competitiveness, but a firm's credit terms are also part of its marketing mix. Customers expect credit, and many firms expect to give it. At issue here is the manner in which Sarah approaches it. The right way is to be firm but reasonable: being 'nasty' to customers is neither necessary nor helpful. It almost certainly means that some customers will go elsewhere as soon as the opportunity arises. So Sarah may be doing more harm than good to the business.

■ Sheila and Manjit think that they have nothing to do with 'the marketing approach' because their job is just to fill shelves. But they are visible to customers, and customers may well ask them questions: their appearance and behaviour are both part of the firm's marketing mix. This customer will not care what their particular job is: she only knows that they represent the supermarket, and that they are unhelpful, unfriendly and lacking in knowledge. Next time she shops, it may be elsewhere. Most retail firms now expect – and train – all their staff how to respond to customers' questions, and the minimum should be to say 'Sorry, I don't know, but I'll find out for you.'

■ Peter is a typical example of a production-oriented person. He needs to rethink his attitude, because if Sally can't sell Peter's output, all the production skills in the world will count for nothing. Furthermore, it is very bad practice to be unhelpful towards colleagues: the best organizations now insist not only that their customers should be treated with every consideration, but that **colleagues should be treated as customers!** Sally makes things worse, by letting the customer see that she is irritated with Peter. The customer will not be impressed with the organization and will have a lingering suspicion about its flexibility and willingness to help.

■ Danny works for a company that has a local monopoly. No matter how much he annoys the neighbours, they cannot get their water from someone else. But incidents like these damage the reputation of a business. On an individual level, they may make customers more inclined to be difficult over all sorts of issues. On a public relations level, a poor reputation can lead to intense opposition to all the company's activities, from its pricing and service policies to its development proposals.

Sarah, Sheila, Manjit, Peter and Danny were not in the front line of the marketing effort. But what they did and said, and how they did and said it, had an effect on their organization's marketing mix. It is important to recognize the following:

■ All employees affect the organization's competitiveness.
■ The way you approach your job, your colleagues and your customers can either help or hinder the marketing effort.

Self-assessment 2

1 Define what is meant by 'the marketing mix'.

_____

_____

_____

2 List **five** factors which usually form an important part of the marketing mix.

_____

_____

_____

_____

_____

3 List **three** 'behind the scenes' factors that can affect long-term customer loyalty.

_____

_____

_____

Answers to these questions can be found on page 78.

4 Summary

- The marketing mix is the sum total of all the factors that make up the organization's 'offer' to its market.

- Every organization has a slightly different marketing mix; otherwise it is difficult to find a competitive edge.

- There are many elements in the marketing mix, but the most important ones are usually:

  - the product itself,
  - the price;
  - the promotional and selling activities;
  - availability;
  - service.

- The marketing mix affects both the customer's initial buying decision and longer-term customer satisfaction, and hence loyalty. This depends largely upon:

  - the performance of the product;
  - behind-the-scenes factors, such as efficiency, service and the attitude of the people involved.

- Customers who complain can become more loyal than before, provided their complaint is dealt with promptly and efficiently.

- The most successful market-led organizations believe that:

  - everyone on the payroll is part of the marketing mix;
  - colleagues should be treated with the same consideration as customers;
  - the way staff approach their job, their colleagues and their customers can either help or hinder the organization's marketing effort.

Session C The right product at the right price

1 Introduction

We have already seen that what counts is what the market wants, not what the supplier thinks it **ought** to want. Any organization that develops a product first, and then seeks a market for it second, is courting disaster.

There are many elements in the marketing mix, and among them the product itself is central. But there are also many different aspects to the product: quality, suitability, design, range and price. Failure to get any one of these right will also threaten the organization's ability to compete.

Above all, the product has to be right for the particular part of the market at which it is aimed.

2 The product

Managers, supervisors and team leaders in all parts of the organization need to gear their efforts to achieving this market success. This is true whether or not they are directly involved in marketing activities.

Activity 18

3 mins

How does an organization know whether its product is meeting the needs of the market? Suggest **three** different ways of finding out.

_____

_____

_____

As you saw in Sessions A and B there are three main ways of knowing whether a product is meeting the needs of its market. The first is simply to look at sales (or take-up, in the case of non-commercial organizations). If sales are on target, clearly the product is meeting the needs of the market. If they are significantly above target, it would be worth finding out why, in order to be able to exploit this success further, and perhaps extend it to other products.

On the other hand, if demand for the product has not matched expectations, or if it is falling, it is not meeting the needs of the market, or not as well as it did before. If sales are stagnating, there is a question mark over the product.

This takes us on to the second source of knowledge: market research. Research can help to show why demand is changing, and whether it is likely to go on doing so.

The third main indicator of how well the product is meeting the needs of the market is feedback from customers, including distributors:

■ positive feedback

in the nature of things, people are more likely to complain about a product they dislike than applaud one they like, but some customers are kind enough to write or phone saying how pleased they are;

■ negative feedback

complaints, returns, cancellations, and similar signs of dissatisfaction.

Organizations should not be afraid of complaints. Any feedback is better than none, and knowing what customers dislike, and where problems may lie, enables them to make improvements sooner rather than later.

People often find it hard to understand why customers are not buying a particular product any longer. There is even a tendency to blame the customers: perhaps they have become less interested in quality, less loyal, even less intelligent.

Of course, this is a fundamental mistake. Change is in the market's very nature:

- the needs of customers change;
- the other products available in the market change;
- all products have a limited life, even when it is a relatively long one.

The market inevitably condemns every product to death, but that doesn't mean that its life cannot be prolonged. Indeed, the first reaction on seeing a product slipping down the charts should be to ask:

- why is it happening?
- what can we do about it?

Activity 19

5 mins

- Grindleford Toys found that, although other product groups were doing well, sales of their high quality cast-metal miniature cars were down around 4.5 per cent compared with the previous year.

Try to list **four** possible explanations for this decline.

_____

_____

_____

_____

The many possible reasons fall into two groups: external factors and internal factors.

2.1 External factors

- Changed economic conditions

If the economy generally has been in recession, all kinds of consumer spending may be affected. Luxury items, and high-quality toys may be in this category, are often the worst affected.

■ Changed market conditions

Customer's needs may have changed without anyone noticing – until someone offers a new product that meets them. But when the right new product comes along, it can suddenly wipe the floor with old-established and highly respected market leaders. In the 1950s, a large majority of toy cars were made of metal. In the 1970s, there was a big switch to plastic, which was much cheaper, although it meant a noticeable drop in quality. More recently, cast metal, with its 'quality feel', has made a comeback. But almost all these products are now made in China, even where the company itself is Europe-based. Global market changes have made relocating production to low-cost countries both technically feasible and administratively convenient.

The most likely explanation for the decline in Grindleford's market is the arrival of new and highly competitive products manufactured abroad.

2.2 Internal factors

It is always possible that internal factors such as the following are responsible for Grindleford's becoming less competitive in the marketplace.

■ Marketing factors

- a failure to market and sell the products effectively;
- a failure to introduce enough new products to replace ageing ones.

■ Management factors

- financial mismanagement;
- a failure to invest in more efficient machinery;
- a failure to streamline working practices;
- poor human relations resulting in low productivity.

■ Production factors

- too many faults and errors in manufacture;
- failure to operate at optimum capacity.

There is little you can do about external factors – you have to learn to live with them. But internal factors are a different matter.

An organization that wishes to keep up with the changing market must be constantly on its toes, and it must be prepared to change its products and its methods of working too. The whole organization needs to be geared to the needs of the ever-changing market.

3 The product range

Most markets can be broken down into segments. These are distinct slices of the market that demand different things from a particular product range.

3.1 Market segmentation and product range

The market for cars is a good example: all cars are basically self-powered boxes for moving people from place to place. However, within the car market there are many distinct needs. Retired people, managing directors, sales reps, first-time buyers, farmers, families and commuters all look for something slightly different. They represent distinct segments of the market. Segmentation is also to do with spending power: what people can afford to buy (and therefore the 'demand' they generate) depends to a large extent on their income. In most markets, there are three broad segments based on income, like this:

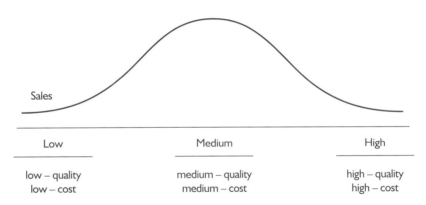

Market segmentation

As you can see from the 'distribution curve' in this diagram, the biggest sales (for most consumer products at any rate) are in the middle ranges, and this is where competition is also highest, because the total sums of money involved here are much greater.

But there is a market at the top end too; this segment produces fewer sales in total, but a relatively high cash income. Profits may also be relatively high here. There is also a market at the bottom end.

Segmentation is a reality. Organizations respond by tailoring their products to these segments. This may involve developing a wide product range that mirrors a wide range of market segments. Thus, Ford offers a wide range of cars, from small 'economy' models to large luxurious ones, and including 'people movers' and off-road vehicles. Many firms prefer to concentrate their efforts on specific sectors: the Italian firm Lamborghini only operates in the top end of the luxury segment, while Fiat concentrates on the lower and middle segments.

35

We can see the same process of matching the product range to market segments in a service indusrty like the restaurant trade.

Restaurant	Description	Market segment
'Le Chapeau Noir'	One of the top restaurants in the country, offering a wide range of individually prepared dishes cooked by internationally famous chefs. Situated in a pleasant rural location and with a very high standard of service.	**Top of the range:** ■ top quality; ■ maximum choice; ■ high prices; ■ small market.
'The Merry Chef'	Part of a nationwide chain, which offers a standardized menu at moderate prices and is organized for maximum cost-efficiency. Situated mainly in busy town centres and providing a medium level of service.	**Middle of the range:** ■ middle quality; ■ limited choice; ■ competitive prices; ■ large market.
'Sid's Cafe'	A family-run café/snack bar, offering tea, coffee and fried meals of the bacon-egg-sausage-chips-and-peas type. Situated on the edge of an industrial estate.	**Bottom of the range:** ■ low quality; ■ limited choice; ■ low prices; ■ small market.

Activity 20

The three different restaurants are clearly aimed at three different market segments, in that they aim to attract three entirely different types of customer. How would you describe the three different types of customer?

Le Chapeau Noir

_____

_____

The Merry Chef

_____

_____

Sid's Cafe

_____

_____

One way of looking at the differences is by social class. Sid's clientele are likely to be working class; the top-of-the-range restaurant attracts the upper class; and the Merry Chef Inn is in between.

The advertising and marketing industry is interested in these distinctions, because what can be marketed successfully to one cannot necessarily be marketed to the others. You may already know that the industry often refers to these groups by a letter:

A   professionals;
B   managers and other senior grades;
C1   white collar workers;
C2   skilled manual workers;
D   unskilled manual workers.

However, this is a very crude division, and it is becoming much more common to try to analyse consumers in more sensitive ways, for example:

- by the area in which they live (for example through the Area Classification of Residential Neighbourhood or ACORN system);
- according to their tastes, interests and lifestyles (e.g. by finding out which newspapers they read, the type of holidays they take and the kind of cars they drive).

Either way, the two principal respects in which the segments differ are:

- the amount they have available to spend;
- their needs in terms of quality;
- the amount of time they have available.

Some restaurants are capable of competing in more than one segment of the market. Many Chinese restaurants, for example, have three different products aimed at three distinct segments within the market for Chinese meals:

- the basic low-cost 'business lunch' for working people in a hurry;
- the full-menu evening meal, a more leisurely affair with a higher standard of service and 'trimmings';
- the take-away and home delivery service.

So Chinese restaurants have a product range that consists of three products. Note that 'product' refers to the type of meal, not the individual items a customer buying a meal will actually choose from.

Activity 21

2 mins

Why is it to the advantage of a restaurant to compete in three separate market segments rather than just one? Note down **one** good reason.

_____

_____

Working in several market segments is also a matter of spreading risk. If an organization meets problems in one segment and makes a loss, there is a good chance that the others will still produce enough profit to keep the business afloat.

It is a simple matter of economics. Restaurants have a particular set of resources – human skills, equipment etc. If they can utilize these same resources across three market segments instead of one, they are both increasing their revenue and reducing their unit costs. It is far more profitable than concentrating on just one part of the market. The same is true of almost any sector of the market. However, where the segments in a market differ greatly, firms may prefer to concentrate on the segments where they have expertise. Rolls-Royce is unlikely to try to enter the market segment that buys cheap run-abouts.

Market segmentation makes sense for service and non-profit providers as well as commercial firms in the manufacturing sector.

■ Wetlands Hospital Trust ran a typical NHS general hospital, treating the usual range of disorders in the usual ways. Management decided to look for ways of developing segmentation within the 'offer to customers'. It was immediately obvious that the hospital had two distinct kinds of customer – the family doctors who referred patients to it (many, but not all, fundholding practices that had contracts with the hospital), and the patients themselves.

Management decided to start with the 'hotel services' provided to in-patients. As well as the 'standard service' in wards containing bays of six to eight beds each, they offered individual rooms for people prepared to pay for more privacy. Beyond this they created a 'private wing' where the level of service – and the fees – were still higher. Thus a range of products was created, in which 'a better hotel service' was offered to those able and willing to pay more.

The medical service remained the same for everyone. However, a product range which in reality had doctors as its customers was gradually developed. The segments were based on speed of service for non-urgent investigations and treatment. At the top was a segment for doctors referring private fee-paying patients; these would receive almost immediate attention. Fundholding family doctors would receive a middle-range service for the patients they referred. At the bottom would be non-fundholders, whose patients would be put on longer waiting lists with no priority.

This particular segmentation was not formally announced due to uncertainty about public reactions and the possible political 'fall-out'.

Activity 22

20 mins

This Activity may provide the basis of appropriate evidence for your S/NVQ portfolio. If you are intending to take this course of action, it might be better to write your answers on separate sheets of paper.

Think about the range of products (or one of the ranges, if there are several) that your own organization offers. These will be products of a similar type, but aimed at different segments of the market, and will draw on the same basic skills and other resources. Analyse the range in terms of price and quality.

1 Arrange them in order from low quality/price through to high quality/price. If there is a large number, choose **not more than five** that represent distinct price/quality levels.

2 Note down what kinds of customers each product in the range is expected to sell to. (You may need to consult whoever specializes in marketing about this.) This will establish what market segments each product is aimed at.

3 Research some price and sales or uptake figures for the range of products you have identified:

- average sale price for each product;
- average number of units sold per month (or per quarter or per year, if more convenient);
- average gross profit margin for each product.

4 Calculate:

a the total sales value;
b the total gross profit that each product returns on average in the period you have chosen.

5 Present some of your figures graphically:

- pie charts showing:
  a each product's share of total sales by unit;
  b each product's share of total gross profit;
- a chart showing average number of units by sales price per unit.

When you have done all this, consider what you have learned about the way market segmentation works in your organization. Are there any gaps in the range? Where is demand biggest? Are there products in the range that are generating so little activity that they may not be worthwhile?

Try to discuss these issues with someone who has marketing or financial responsibilities. What is the thinking behind the range as it presently stands. What plans, if any, are there to change it? What suggestions for improvement can you contribute?

39

3.2 Range and choice

Simple economics is not the only reason for offering a range of products; it is also important to be able to offer customers a choice. Often this means providing relatively minor variations within each product in the range, as in the case of the Chinese restaurant.

For another example, take a confectionery wholesaler that distributes its products to high street retailers.

To persuade the retailers to do business with them, the wholesaler must be able to offer what the retailers believe their market wants. In this case, it is variety: a range of different brands, types, flavours, colours and sizes from which to choose.

Retailers will insist on the wholesaler supplying the full range of products and maintaining their availability at all times. This will have a big impact on the way the wholesaler approaches its business, and in turn on the manufacturers from which it acquires its supplies.

Activity 23

Suppose you want to buy someone a waterproof outdoor coat as a birthday present. Near where you live, but five miles apart, are two factory shops where you can buy the kind of coat you are looking for.

Factory A makes only one kind of outdoor coat. It is good value at £49.99, but is only available in green.

Factory B offers a range of coats, in a variety of styles and qualities, with prices ranging from £39.99 to £125.99.

If you had time to visit only one of the shops, which would you choose, and why?

_____

_____

_____

_____

You may have had a particular reason for choosing Factory A, but most people would have plumped for Factory B. The reason must be obvious: choice. In this case:

- a choice of prices;
- a choice of qualities;
- a choice of colours and styles.

The same goes for cars: we want a choice of colours, finishes, engine sizes and accessories. And even in business markets, such as for office furniture, computers, catering services and packaging materials, the customer appreciates being offered a choice and is unlikely to be impressed by suppliers who do not offer it.

But giving the customers the choice they demand can be hard work for people throughout the supplying organization. It usually means:

- developing a range of lines – and thus more time and money spent on research, design, scheduling, setting up machines, training people and so on;
- maintaining a range of stock and a variety of facilities – and thus more time and money spent on warehousing, keeping inventory records, recording stock movements and other overheads.

4 The right price

Of all the factors which make up the marketing mix, price is usually the most important. At the time of writing, the British beef industry was in a very deep recession as a result of fears of 'mad cow disease'. In order to stimulate demand, butchers and supermarkets slashed prices by 50 per cent or more. Only these deep price cuts were capable of generating demand, and even then the level of sales was some 30 per cent below what it had been a few months previously.

In principle, anything will sell (i.e. there will be demand for anything) if the price falls low enough. Scrap metal is a case in point. Even a rusty and broken-down washing machine, which will never work again, can be sold for scrap for a small sum.

The problem with most goods and services is that the price has to be low enough to create a demand, but high enough to produce a profit, and it is difficult to get this right.

4.1 Costing a product

To produce a profit, the price of a product must produce a revenue that is greater than the total costs involved in getting it to the customer.

Activity 24

3
mins

List **six** main types of cost which go into a product like Grindleford's metal toys from the case study on page 33.

_____

_____

_____

_____

_____

_____

The main costs associated with a manufactured product are generally these:

- Development costs, including:

  - market research;
  - design and pre-production costs;
  - making dies and jigs;
  - test-runs.

- Direct production costs, including:

  - set-up costs;
  - materials (metal, paint, rubber);
  - components bought in;
  - packaging;
  - repairs and maintenance to machinery etc.;
  - wages and salaries of production staff;
  - energy.

- Indirect (overhead) costs, including:

  - management costs;
  - administrative costs (including wages and salaries of office staff);
  - rent, rates etc.;
  - lighting, heating etc.;
  - telephone, post, couriers etc.;
  - insurance, legal fees etc.;
  - training.

- Distribution and selling costs, including:

  - storage and transport costs;
  - advertising and costs of promotional events;
  - promotional literature;
  - salaries of selling staff;
  - travel and other expenses.

There may be many more incidental costs than I have listed, and there also has to be a margin for profit; and probably something for tax.

The simplest way to work out the price of a product is to add up all the anticipated costs and then add a percentage for profit. (The costing of service products is broadly similar, except that materials and 'production' costs are usually insignificant, while labour costs are considerably higher.)

This is the so-called 'cost-plus' method. However, this method is based entirely on internal considerations, especially production; it takes no account whatsoever of the market.

4.2 Pricing for the market

- Grindleford's worked out that a new model aimed at the middle segment of the market would cost £3.41 to make, on a production run of 10,000. Fifteen per cent would be added as a profit margin, bringing the price at which it could be supplied to retailers to £3.92. Retailers would then add their own margin, and the model would probably appear in the shops at £4.99.

Activity 25

3 mins

Perhaps this is not the right price for the product. What other considerations would Grindleford's have to bear in mind when setting a price? Try to think of **two**.

_____

_____

The price may be right from Grindleford's point of view, but is it right for the market? They need to consider how it compares with the prices of competing products. If the competition sells at £3.99, how can this product sell at £4.99?

A market-led firm would have approached this from a different angle: 'At what price can we sell this product? OK, now how can we produce the product at that price?'

If the answer is 'We can't', then it is a waste of time and money even trying.

This is the Japanese approach, which has proved so successful in recent years: find out what the market wants, and what it is prepared to pay, then produce a product at that price. Since competition is expected to grow every year, every part of the organization is expected to find cost reductions and productivity gains that will maintain or improve the competitive position. This *kaizen* or 'continuous improvement' approach is becoming widely accepted throughout the world.

Activity 26

3 mins

There is no reason in principle why Grindleford's products should not sell, at a higher price, in the top segment of the market, provided they are right for that segment. What would 'right' be in this context?

_____

_____

_____

_____

A product that survives in the upper end of the market must have something about it that justifies the higher price, for example:

- superior quality and durability;
- a high reputation and a quality brand name;
- superior style and fashion.

In other words, it has to be a 'premium product'.

5 Product quality

As you have seen, the quality of a product:

- is clearly part of the marketing mix;
- is closely related to the price which can be charged.

However, this does not mean that every product has to be of the highest possible quality. If that were true, all cars would have to be Rolls-Royces.

What it does mean is that the quality has to be right for the price charged. This explains why in most markets you find a range of goods which do the same job but at different levels of price and sophistication. It also accounts for the fact that customers do not expect Rolls-Royce standards from a Skoda, but can still be perfectly happy with the Skoda.

Problems arise when the quality falls below **what the customer expects for the price paid**, and when the back-up services do not meet the customer's expectations.

5.1 Maintaining standards of quality

■ Lee & Sherrills, a leading food manufacturer, were able to buy ground almonds from a number of countries and via various different suppliers, with very little variation in price. As it happened, they normally bought them from Turkey, through a supplier with whom they had a good relationship. Then problems began to arise. One consignment had to be rejected because it was contaminated with chlorine. Next, the colour of the product changed from white to a pale beige. Finally, there were hold-ups when the supplier was unable to deliver on time.

L&S were reluctant to abandon their old-established supplier and pressed them for guarantees of quality and supply for the future, but these did not solve the problems. So they simply switched to another source, and the original supplier lost the account, even though they offered to drop the price.

Activity 27

2 mins

Contracts can easily be lost owing to production problems. What would you say were the supplier's **two** major shortcomings?

_____

_____

_____

_____

First, they did not monitor the production quality properly. Someone must have known that the quality was falling, but nothing was done about it. Second, they failed to meet the customer's delivery dates. It is easy for suppliers to become sloppy about this, but if the customer needs everything exactly at the right time in order to start a production run, then it is a major problem.

There was also a third problem – the supplier did not put things right when the customer complained.

Quality usually means reliability too. Lee & Sherrills' original supplier lost their contract because they became unreliable. Most commercial customers place a value on reliability and consistency and are prepared to pay more for it. This is another pointer to how managers, supervisors and team leaders in all areas of an organization can help the marketing effort.

5.2 The quality of service products

The nature of the product offered by service-based organizations is also important. For example, pre-privatization British Rail had many critics for many reasons, but one particular area of complaint used to be passenger enquiries. People phoning up to check train times often had to wait for long periods before getting an answer. Sometimes the phone seemed permanently engaged, sometimes it just rang and rang – in fact, it was common for customers to give up in disgust. When the phone was answered, the people at the other end often seemed brusque and unhelpful.

The enquiry staff themselves were probably pretty unhappy: feeling overworked, understaffed and generally misunderstood. They probably felt they were doing their best to provide a decent service, but that customers didn't appreciate the difficulties they faced.

Activity 28

What do you think could be done to improve a service of that kind?

_____

_____

_____

BR's answer to these problems was to increase staffing levels, install more 'phone lines and train the enquiry staff to be more friendly and helpful. Now a service which was a constant irritant to customers has become a cause for much praise, a very positive element in BR's marketing mix.

And why was the improvement made? Simply because the people concerned started to look at it from the customer's point of view.

There is an important lesson here:

customers are not interested in your problems – they simply want the right product at the right time.

Here is another example of how service quality affects the customer's attitude.

■ Janet was office supervisor for a firm of architects. One Monday morning in January she found that the special machine used for outputting large-scale architectural drawings from the computer database was not working.

The senior partner urgently needed to output three important drawings, which he had been altering over the weekend. Janet phoned their usual equipment maintenance people and tried to explain her problem. An uninterested voice interrupted her to say: 'Don't worry, it's the cold you know. It'll sort itself out. Give us a ring back at lunchtime if it doesn't and we'll see what we can do.'

Janet then searched through the *Yellow Pages* and found another maintenance firm. An interested voice assured her that they would be able to help and then listened while she explained her problem.

'It's probably not a serious fault, just the cold weather. Some machines can be affected like that. Try to get some heat onto the machine – just gentle heat or you may do some damage. In the meantime I'll re-route one of our service engineers, so there should be someone there within the hour.'

Activity 29

Write down a few of the words that you might use to describe the approach of the two firms that Janet tried.

The original firm:

_____

_____

The new firm:

_____

_____

I think most experts would make a judgement like this:

■ the original firm: inefficient, couldn't-care-less, useless, disorganized, complacent, sloppy;
■ the new firm: efficient, helpful, concerned, organized, keen – and willing to 'go the extra mile' to please a customer.

The original firm is likely to be on the way out; the newcomers may have won a new account.

47

If you are involved in the production, delivery or quality control of any product or service of any kind, think carefully about this issue.

What can you do:

- to make sure you not only meet the customer's needs in terms of quality, but go further to ensure complete satisfaction?
- to make sure your product always reaches the customer on time?

Self-assessment 3

10 mins

1   List **two** external factors that can reduce an organization's competitiveness:

_____

_____

2   Complete this sentence in your own words:

The selling price of a product has to be low enough to _____

but high enough to _____ _____ _____.

3   Explain what is meant by 'a segment of the market'.

_____

_____

_____

4   Describe the cost-plus method of costing a product.

_____

_____

_____

5   What is the main shortcoming of the cost-plus method?

_____

_____

_____

Answers to these questions can be found on page 79.

6 Summary

- All products have a limited life-cycle, but their useful life can be prolonged.

- A product's decline may be due to:

  - external factors (changed economic or market conditions);
  - internal factors (such as inefficiency or lack of investment).

- Most organizations try to offer a range of products to the market. This brings in extra revenues by using the same basic skills and material resources.

- The range of products is designed to match different segments of the market, which are defined mainly by:

  - the amount they have to spend;
  - their needs in terms of quality.

- All things being equal, customers tend to prefer the supplier who offers them the widest choice. This is another reason for offering a range of products.

- Anything will sell if the price falls low enough. The art of pricing is to set a price which is:

  - high enough to make a profit;
  - low enough to create a demand.

- The simplest method of working out the price of a product is to add up all the costs involved and then add a margin for profit. This is the cost-plus method.

- The problem with this method is that it takes no account of what the market is prepared to pay.

- High-priced products can still sell, provided that they can justify being a premium product.

- Maintaining a consistent quality is vital for success in the market.

- Customers prefer a reliable product from a reliable supplier.

- Quality and consistency are just as important for organizations whose products are services.

Session D The right place, the right time and the right way

1 Introduction

Suppose you have the right product at the right price, but you offer it to the market a year late (or, just as bad, a year early). Obviously, you will miss the boat.

On the other hand, suppose you have the right product, at the right price and at the right time, but you launch it, say, in East Anglia only, when the real market is the whole of Northern Europe. Again, you will miss the boat.

These two suppositions may be extreme, but it is surprising how often organizations fail to hit the right time and place for their products. There may be all sorts of reasons for this, from failure to study the market accurately, to development problems, to sheer bad luck. But whatever the reason, the upshot is a disaster.

In this part of the workbook you will find out more about why the right place and time are so crucial, and look at some of the things that organizations – and that means the people in them – can do to make sure things go right.

2 The right place

Perhaps you had cereal for breakfast today, or perhaps a cup of coffee and a slice of toast. Whatever it was, it's unlikely that you produced these things yourself. The raw materials probably came from overseas, perhaps from the other side of the globe, and even the factory that processed them may have been hundreds of miles away. In order for you to buy them, they had to be brought to a place where you could conveniently do so. The same applies to the customers who buy the products that we ourselves supply.

Making sure that goods and services are available when the customer wants to buy them is part of marketing, and comes under the general heading of **distribution**.

51

Two hundred years ago, people in countries like Britain were fairly self-sufficient. Their needs were simple — mainly food, clothing and basic tools and equipment — and most they could either produce themselves or get from a fairly local source. Now our needs are much more complex and we produce very little for our own direct use. The way we live is utterly dependent on world-wide markets and a system of distribution that brings us what we demand from the ends of the earth if necessary.

You can think of distribution in two main ways:

- the chain of distribution;
- physical distribution.

These obviously refer to goods rather than services, but the distribution of service products is similarly important. So too is the storage and handling of the stocks prior to delivery.

2.1   The chain of distribution

The 'chain of production and distribution' looks like this:

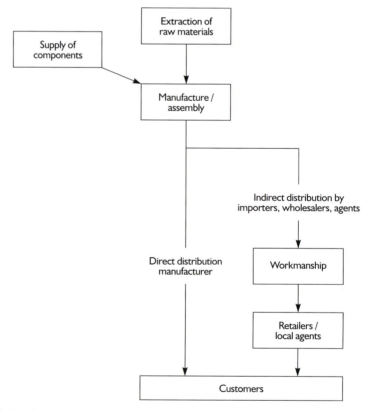

Chain of distribution

This chain may have few links or many, but if even one of them fails, the customer's needs will not be met, and he or she will go elsewhere.

2.2 Stock handling and storage

Since warehousing plays an important part in the chain of distribution, the efficiency of stock handling and storage obviously affects the ability to supply the right product at the right place and time.

Here is an example of what can go wrong.

■ Mary, the supervisor in an office equipment company, received an order for a white leather executive chair, reference number 2140. She checked with the stock records, which showed one such chair in stock.

Mary passed the order down to the warehouse supervisor, who phoned back to say that bin 2140 was empty. As the order was for urgent delivery, the customer cancelled it.

Later that day, Mary was walking through the warehouse on her way to the canteen, when she spotted what she thought was a white leather chair type 2140 perched on top of a bin containing desks. She had a word with one of the warehouse staff, who explained that a colleague had put the chair there three weeks previously because bin 2140 was full at the time.

Activity 30

3 mins

What was the problem in this case, and who was responsible?

_____

_____

_____

The problem was lack of communication – the warehouse staff didn't communicate what they had done. But the responsibility was the warehouse supervisor's:

■ for not ensuring that his staff realized they needed to communicate about such things;
■ perhaps for not encouraging an atmosphere in which people were willing to communicate;
■ and certainly for not carrying out spot checks on bin contents.

This incident illustrates just some of the problems of place and time which arise every day in the handling, storage and control of stock. The supervisor is often the person best able to solve these problems.

It's no good producing the right product at the right price, if we cannot get it to the customer at the right time.

2.3 Physical distribution

Then there is the transport side, the physical distribution: the process of sending the products down the chain from one location to another, until they reach the customer.

Physical delivery of the product is an extremely important part of the marketing mix. Indeed, under contract law, the buyer has the right to make delivery terms a condition of the contract; and if the delivery is late, they can refuse payment and even sue for damages. Moreover, you're likely to lose that customer to another supplier.

In recent years, customers' delivery needs have tightened up. Many manufacturers and retailers now operate a 'just-in-time' system for deliveries of goods. This means that the goods should be timed to arrive just before they are needed, no later, and never much earlier. Thus, supermarkets expect that delivery vans will arrive at a particular time, so that their staff can be ready to check the goods and move them straight onto the shelves on the shop floor.

Manufacturers expect parts and sub-assemblies to arrive precisely when they are needed on the assembly line.

Activity 31

4 mins

What do you think is the main advantage of the just-in-time system to retailers and manufacturers?

_____

_____

The principal advantage for the customer is having to hold only a very small amount of stock. Stock costs money, and it needs space to house it and people to look after it. It also ties up money until the moment when the stock is actually sold.

Activity 32

3 mins

What disadvantages does a just-in-time delivery system have for the supplier? Write down **two** suggestions.

_____

_____

Next time you are in a large supermarket, sneak a look into the stock room. You'll find that it's surprisingly small. Supermarkets store their stock on the shelves: their aim is to sell it, not warehouse it. The stock room is mainly used for storing 'faulty returns', goods delivered in error and extra stocks required for special promotions.

Customers such as supermarkets work long hours and have a high throughput, and they may require deliveries to be made at any time of day or night. This means that the supplier's staff, and especially despatch staff and drivers, also have to match these hours, which may be inconvenient for them.

It also means that, in effect, the supplier does the warehousing for the customer, and thus carries the cost of that operation.

Third, the system means more frequent and generally smaller deliveries, because the customer is no longer prepared to store more than a minimum of stock.

Suppliers often grumble about all this, but at the end of the day they have no choice. There is always competition, and if one supplier cannot, or will not, deliver at the right place and the right time, then someone else certainly will.

Meeting delivery needs within the narrow time-frame often demanded calls for hard work and attention to detail.

■ Samuelsons produce hot pre-packed meals, which they distribute to offices, shops and factories over a wide area, using a small fleet of vans. Orders are accepted up to 11 am on the day they are required, and all orders are delivered by arrangement between 12 noon and 2 pm.

Activity 33

5 mins

Jot down **four** of the things that Samuelsons would have to do to make sure that their customers got what they wanted at the right time and place. (Don't worry about the product itself – you can assume they have got the raw materials, equipment and so on.)

_____

_____

_____

_____

All sorts of things could go wrong with a time-sensitive operation like this. Some of the most important areas are as follows:

- ensure that all orders have correct consignment notes so that they go to the right address;
- double-check that each consignment is actually what the customer ordered;
- make sure the orders are properly packed so that they don't get spilled or contaminated;
- plan the most effective routes for the vehicles;
- make sure the drivers are properly trained and instructed;
- make sure the vehicles are regularly serviced and repaired so as to minimize the risk of breakdowns;
- make sure the vehicles meet legal requirements so that they aren't kept off the road unnecessarily;
- make sure there is a vehicle and driver on stand-by in case of emergencies.

Similar points will apply to almost any organization which operates a distribution service. All these things need to be done by the people behind the scenes in order to support the marketing operation. The market demands a service that is economical, but also reliable; customers soon get tired of receiving their orders late or not at all!

2.4 Distribution of services

Service-based organizations are not necessarily concerned with distributing goods; but they do have to make sure that the service they offer is 'delivered' to the customer. A healthcare organization, for example, needs to ensure that its services are made available to everyone in its catchment area, and that they can gain access to it with the minimum of difficulty.

Activity 34

4 mins

- Wetlands District Council's customers are the people who live and work in the district. It provides them with numerous services, such as refuse collection, street lighting, road maintenance, council housing, housing benefits and schools.

What would be involved in making a service like housing benefit advice available at the right place and time? Write down **two** or **three** suggestions.

The first issue is informing the customers that the service exists. This is much harder than one might imagine. Even when it is something that would be to people's advantage, it takes a big commitment of time, money and energy to push 'awareness' beyond the 50 per cent level.

The next step is to make it easy for the customers to gain access to the service. In recent years, councils have tried to achieve this by such means as:

- providing free telephone 'advice-lines' for use by the public;
- offering advice outside normal hours, for example in the evening and at weekends;
- breaking up the housing department into smaller units and siting these locally, near where the tenants actually live;
- fitting out lorries or buses as mobile advice centres and touring the localities on pre-advertised dates;
- sending council officers to visit customers in their homes.

This sort of thing is not yet universal, but it is a clear sign that local authorities and similar organizations are adopting a marketing approach towards the services they supply.

3 The right time

Right for the customer, that is. This may or may not correspond with 'as soon as we can do it without disruption to our usual way of doing things'.

3.1 'I want it now!'

Time often gives one supplier the competitive edge.

> Commercial markets plan ahead and usually seek fixed dates for delivery well in advance. Early delivery is often a nuisance rather than a benefit. Consumer markets are different. Customers often want their new purchase instantly and feel frustrated if this isn't possible. Anyone who has ever ordered a three-piece suite will know the feeling.

- Ramiz wanted to buy a new computer. This is how he decided between the twenty or so possible suppliers:

  - he worked out the exact specifications he wanted;
  - he listed the suppliers who could provide exactly that;
  - he checked the prices by telephone and shortlisted three;
  - he then checked how soon they could deliver and chose the quickest.

All other things being equal, the time factor gave one supplier the competitive edge (and indeed the computer arrived exactly when they promised). This firm was well-managed and well-organized, and everyone working there gave top priority to the customer's needs: that's why it got the business.

Activity 35

■ Wetlands District Council was seeking tenders for the installation of a new computer system in its main offices. It shortlisted three different suppliers.

Supplier A was cheap, but would need 'about nine months' to complete the installation. Supplier B was mid-priced, and would also need nine months to complete the installation, but gave a cast-iron guarantee that the work would be completed on time. Supplier C was more expensive, but offered to complete the work in seven months.

Which one would you choose, all other things being equal? Give the reasons for your choice.

_____

_____

_____

_____

A difficult choice, because we do not know how much weight this customer would place on time as opposed to money. On the whole, the best choice is probably Supplier B, because it is better to be sure about completion **within a given time** than **unsure** about a somewhat earlier time.

■ Harry was quality control supervisor on a production line making stereo loudspeakers. One day the sales manager came in and told him that batch number 9193 (fifty pairs of speakers for export) must be ready by 4 pm the following day, as they had to be delivered to the airport six hours later. (This was three whole days ahead of the normal schedule.)

When the sales manager had gone, Harry said to Joyce, his line manager, 'Sales have gone and done it again, Joyce. All they do is promise customers ridiculous deadlines, and to hell with everything else.'

Activity 36

4 mins

We've all heard comments like Harry's. What points would you make to Harry if you were Joyce? Write your thoughts down in **one** or **two** sentences.

_____

_____

_____

_____

_____

_____

An agreed delivery date is almost always a condition of an order, and sometimes it is the most important condition. Sometimes it is impossible to get the order without being prepared to offer an ultra-short lead time.

Of course, it is always possible for the sales team simply to tell their customer, 'Sorry – we can't do it in the time. It'll mean messing up our routine.' But that is a very plain message to the customer that their order isn't important enough to bother with: next time that customer will go elsewhere.

3.2 Seasonality

The need to supply products at the right time affects the way work is organized, especially where demand fluctuates through the year.

Activity 37

3 mins

John sells soap powder, Mary sells children's toys. What do you think will be the biggest difference between their working lives?

_____

_____

There are several differences you might have written down – for example, toys are a varied and rapidly changing product group, while the range of soap powder is limited and remains much the same year in year out.

Much industrial and commercial activity is also seasonally 'skewed'. Think about: electricity generation; agricultural contracting; hotels; holiday companies; healthcare (winter peaks of bronchitis and 'flu); estate agencies (spring is the busiest time for house sales); construction (winter is a relatively quiet period).

The biggest difference, though, is 'seasonality'. Soap powder sales are only slightly seasonal, dipping a little in the summer months. John will therefore have a steady routine that will not vary much from month to month. Children's toys, on the other hand, are highly seasonal: almost 60 per cent of all retail toy sales take place in the pre-Christmas period.

This means that Mary's activities will be quite different at different times of year. She will probably be extremely busy:

- in January, when the major toy fairs take place and the big retailers are placing their orders for the following Christmas;
- in the middle of the year, when the smaller retailers are placing Christmas orders.

For the rest of the year, pressure of work will be much lower.

Seasonal demand will also influence the way manufacturers organize their work. Anyone who makes seasonal products is likely to find themselves under a great deal of pressure at certain peak times. But it's essential to meet the challenge: otherwise, yet again, a competitor will do so.

Activity 38

6 mins

Write down a list of **ten** consumer products for which demand is highly seasonal.

_____	_____
_____	_____
_____	_____
_____	_____
_____	_____

Suggestions to this Activity can be found on page 80.

A vast variety of goods (and services – for example, restaurants offering facilities for Christmas) fall into the category of seasonal products, and market research plus experience will tell those concerned quite clearly when the peaks are to be expected. However, there can still be unpredictable surges (or slumps) in demand, plus special priority orders. In the face of fierce competition, it is essential to get the product to its destination on time – and the person who decides what is meant by 'on time' is the customer!

4 The right way: promotion

Promotion and selling are the 'sharp end' of the marketing process. In fact, these are the activities that most people think of first when they hear the word 'marketing'. Of course, marketing is a much wider concept, but that does not diminish the importance of 'the right way'.

We may well deliver the right product at the right price to the right place at the right time, but it will not be alone in that marketplace. Skilful competitors will have their own products there, and their marketing mix, though no doubt different from ours, is also designed to be attractive to the customer.

At this stage, the last competitive edge that we have is the skill and initiative of our promotional and selling people.

Promotion

In broad terms, both promotion and selling follow the AIDA strategy. This stands for the processes involved in persuading the customer to buy our product rather than another:

getting their   **A**ttention;
arousing their   **I**nterest in the product;
stimulating a   **D**esire to acquire it;
turning desire into   **A**ction, i.e. a purchase.

As you saw in Session A, promotion is about:

- informing the customer about the product (mainly through advertising);
- encouraging them to choose it.

Promotional techniques used include:

- advertising;
- distributing promotional literature to retail outlets etc.;
- direct mail campaigns;
- organizing promotional activities such as exhibitions;
- public relations; and so on.

All these are about communication, and their purpose is to gain the customers' **attention**, to **interest** them in the goods or services concerned and to start creating a **desire** to buy them.

EXTENSION 3
Promotion is a specialized subject outside the scope of this workbook. If you would like to learn more about it, you could take up this extension.

Sales promotions often feature a 'free gift' or other benefit in addition to the item purchased. Of course, sellers try to minimize the cost of any such attraction to themselves, while exaggerating its 'value' to the customer. One notorious exception was the promotion launched by Hoover in the early 1990s. Hoover offered free flights to the USA with every appliance purchased. Sales boomed, but the demand for the free flights was almost as big. The cost — and the multitude of wrangles with customers as Hoover tried to get it under control — came close to bankrupting the company.

Some promotional activities aim to generate sales directly. This is particularly true of what are called sales promotions – the wide range of financial inducements that are used to encourage people to buy. From the 20p 'money-off' voucher for a packet of coffee to the mail-out that offers £1,000 off the usual price of a two-ton van 'for orders placed before 31 March', these are intended to result in action, not just interest.

In spite of the steady increase in sales promotions and direct selling activities, 'selling' is still a recognizably different kind of activity. As we pointed out in Session A, it involves bringing a human being into the process, to turn interest into action.

5 The right way: selling

Many of us may think of selling as a specialist role, about which the rest of us don't have to worry too much.

Perhaps this is true in some organizations, but there are many cases – such as retailing – where it isn't.

5.1 Selling – the retail sector

Overall the most important form of selling used in retailing does not involve sales staff at all. It is the way the goods are displayed in order to make them as attractive and desirable as possible. This speciality is called merchandising, or, alternatively, 'silent selling'.

Nearly one employed person in every eight works in retailing, and many of them are directly involved in selling.

Of course selling in the retail sector takes different forms:

■ some retail sales staff are expected to **sell actively**, by going up to every customer who enters and working through a sales routine;
■ others are told not to approach customers, but when a customer asks them for help, they are expected to 'close the sale', **encourage** them to buy extra items ('add-on sales') or buy a higher-priced alternative ('selling up');
■ the majority of retail staff do not sell actively, but are expected to **make it easier for customers to buy** by being polite, helpful and informative.

Obviously, supervisors have a key role to play in all three situations, because they are responsible for giving a good example and making sure that the sales staff perform their selling tasks effectively.

Activity 39

If you have never worked in retailing you may not have realized that these different selling strategies existed, but if you think about your own experiences as a shopper, you will soon recognize them. Try to give **one** example of each of the following types of retail firm.

In Type 1, staff sell actively by approaching customers.

_____

In Type 2, staff sell, but only after customers approach them.

_____

In Type 3, staff only have to help customers buy.

_____

Some examples can be found on page 80.

5.2 Selling – the salesforce method

But what about all those organizations where the selling is done by sales representatives who go 'out on the road'? Many people sell cars, insurance or double glazing directly to consumers, but the bulk of the professional representatives work for the industrial, commercial and service sectors, selling to organizations, not individuals.

As you saw in Session A, the representative has several roles to fulfil. Being a two-way channel of communication between the company and its customers is one of the important ones. Identifying potential new customers is another.

Most important, however, is selling: persuading the customer to buy. This process will typically involve:

- projecting an honest, competent and confident image;
- identifying what satisfactions the customer is seeking and presenting the product in these terms;
- dealing with objections (the customer's arguments for not finalizing the sale, whether expressed or not);
- negotiating the price and other details;
- 'closing the sale'.

All this demands special skills, including communication (including using modern presentation techniques), negotiation and sales-specific skills such as being able to 'close' the sale. These are professional skills: they have to be learned, and they grow with experience.

At one time, the travelling representative was typically a 'loner', mobile, on the road for long periods and depending on his or her wits. This picture is a lot less true today. Most organizations think in terms of a sales team, in which a number of individuals, each with their own specialities, work together. They will try to build a relationship with a potential customer, win their confidence and then turn this into sales.

■ Busaco Materials was a newly formed UK subsidiary of a large Spanish supplier of building materials and equipment. It set up a sales team to try to carve itself out a market with UK building contractors. The team consisted of:

- Emma, a 'PA/secretary' whose job was to answer the phone, greet visitors and output correspondence, faxes and e-mails;
- Rahul, who processed orders and chased deliveries;
- Michael, the sales manager, in charge of the team as a whole;
- Isabella, accountant/estimator, responsible for preparing quotations for customers, and the only Spanish member of the team;
- Geoff, whose title was 'sales researcher': it was his job to find out when major new building projects were planned and to maintain a database on customers and competitors;
- Dorothy, sales executive; her job was to make initial contact with potential customers, to arrange sales presentations with them and to handle routine contacts thereafter; about half her time was spent out of the office.

A sales presentation would be attended by Michael, Isabella and Dorothy. Dorothy would prepare a slide show or computer-based presentation, plus other literature, and she and Michael would do most of the talking. If things went well, Michael would negotiate the details of the contract, with Isabella's help. Thereafter, Dorothy, Rahul and Geoff would be left to get on with things, under Michael's general supervision.

Portfolio of evidence AI.3, DI.I	**Activity 40**	 20 mins

This Activity may provide the basis of appropriate evidence for your S/NVQ portfolio. If you are intending to take this course of action, it might be better to write your answers on separate sheets of paper.

This Activity involves you in analysing the sales function in your own organization, or one that you know well. In particular, you will be looking at how the various people involved in selling work together as a team – and what their individual roles are.

You will need to talk to at least some of the people concerned. When you have done so, draw up a list of the team members and describe what role each plays.

Then make notes on how they work together to:

- decide how the 'sales pitch' will be put together;
- identify potential customers;
- make the initial contact;
- prepare for and handle sales meetings, presentations etc.;
- follow-up sales contacts.

Bear in mind that every organization will arrange its selling activities slightly differently. Some may well involve non-sales specialists like yourself in selling activities. You could also put forward your own proposals for improving the current set-up.

5.3 Back-up: caring for the customer

To do their job efficiently and effectively, the salesforce depends heavily on the support they get from their colleagues in the organization. Without this support, they may be unable to satisfy the customers' expectations and need – in both the short and the long term.

Activity 41

What can a team supervisor in an office cleaning firm do to back up the efforts of the sales reps as they visit potential clients?

_____
_____
_____
_____

Back-up might take many forms:

- the reps may need information, as in the third example in Activity 17;
- they may need schedules or price lists posted out;
- they may want a supervisor to talk directly to the customer about some technical or procedural point.

At some stage, the customer may want to talk directly to the workteam, to try to judge how skilled and reliable they are. And the supervisor is highly likely to be involved in this.

But there is also a general point to make here: whenever you are in contact with people outside your organization, whether these are customers or not, you should always try to give the best possible impression. Another workbook in the series, *Caring for the Customer*, deals with customer-related aspects of marketing.

This returns us to the central issue of this workbook – the idea that in a modern, market-led organization, everyone on the payroll is part of the marketing mix, and that everyone can either help or hinder the marketing effort.

What do you do to 'sell' your organization? In the broadest possible sense we are all responsible for selling our organization, by:

- helping to give it a good public image by our own behaviour;
- taking every opportunity to help the marketing effort;
- being positive about the product;
- being supportive of the efforts of colleagues to develop the business.

In the world of the competitive market, it's the only way to survive.

Self-assessment 4

10 mins

Comment briefly on the following statements.

1 Distribution is a technical matter and has nothing to do with the marketing approach.

_____

_____

2 The chain of distribution can have many links or few.

_____

_____

3 Just-in-time delivery systems are highly inconvenient for the supplier and should be avoided.

_____

_____

4   Time is seldom a crucial part of the marketing mix because most customers allow plenty of lead time.

_____

_____

5   The old saying 'time is money' has little meaning today.

_____

_____

6   Distribution is not really an issue for service-type products such as security, office cleaning and insurance.

_____

_____

7   In terms of the marketing mix, the right place is always more important than the right time.

_____

_____

8   Customers should be realistic about delivery lead times and accept that producers can't keep disrupting production plans for their benefit.

_____

_____

9   Promotion is an activity which is best left to the specialists.

_____

_____

10   Everyone in an organization can help its marketing effort.

_____

_____

Answers to these questions can be found on pages 79–80.

6 Summary

- It is no good having the right product at the right price if it isn't made available at the right place and the right time.

- The mechanism for getting manufactured products to the customer at the right place and time is the chain of production and distribution, which includes:

  - stock handling and storage;
  - physical distribution.

- Customers are becoming more demanding in terms of distribution and delivery.

- Service products also have to be distributed to the customer, though the means of doing so are different.

- Time is often a decisive element in the marketing mix.

- Responsibility for ensuring that the product reaches the customer at the right place and time is shared by everybody working in:

  - sales;
  - administration;
  - production;
  - distribution.

- Managers, supervisors and team leaders have a particular responsibility to ensure that all their staff work towards this goal.

- Promotion and selling are the final important elements in the marketing mix. They can provide the competitive edge when a number of equally good products confront each other in the market place.

- Promotion is about using techniques to attract the customers' attention and arouse their interest.

- Selling is about personal skills to turn the customers' interest into action (i.e. a sale).

- In organizations where the selling is carried out by a specialized salesforce, other staff can still assist and provide back-up.

- In the final analysis, everyone in an organization has a role to play in helping the product to succeed.

Performance checks

Jot down the answers to the following questions on *Marketing and Selling*.

Question 1   How would you define the term 'the market'?

_____

_____

Question 2   Why is it necessary for businesses to keep bringing new products onto the market?

_____

_____

Question 3   Define 'marketing'.

_____

_____

Question 4   What do we mean by the term 'the marketing approach'?

_____

_____

Question 5   What is the basic role of market research?

_____

_____

Question 6   What does it mean when we say an organization is 'product-led'?

_____

_____

Question 7   What do we mean by the term 'the marketing mix'?

_____

_____

Question 8   What is special about a 'premium' product?

_____

_____

69

Question 9   Why do many organizations try to offer their markets a range of products at different levels of price?

_____

_____

Question 10   When you have worked out how much a product will cost to produce, what else do you have to do in order to set a selling price?

_____

_____

Question 11   What would the chain of production and distribution be for a TV assembled in the UK from a mixture of UK and foreign components.

_____

_____

Question 12   Why should non-commercial organizations consider adopting a marketing approach?

_____

_____

Question 13   What is the likely result of failing to get all the elements of the marketing mix right?

_____

_____

Question 14   What is the meaning of the letters AIDA?

_____

_____

_____

_____

Question 15   What's missing from this formula:

The right product, at the right price, at the right place, at the right time.

_____

Answers to these questions can be found on pages 81–2.

2 Workbook assessment

Read the following case study and then deal with the questions that follow. Write your answers on a separate sheet of paper.

■ UK Flowlight is a regional distributor of solid fuels. It has small sales offices in about twenty towns, four depots and an administrative office in Corby. The total workforce is about eighty, of whom roughly two-thirds are part-timers.

The company was traditionally a coal merchant. Until the 1970s, its main products were home deliveries of coal for open fires and coke for boilers. In 1974 it still had 480 employees, but drastic market changes were in the offing. New laws on smoke emissions, industrial disputes in the coal industry and an increasing switch away from open fires towards gas central heating reduced the domestic solid fuels market by an average of 3 per cent a year. The market is now only one-third of what it was in 1974, and the company has shrunk steadily.

Now its main products are various smokeless fuels; regular delivery runs cover the area from Derby in the north to Oxford in the south, and from Worcester and Shrewsbury in the west as far as King's Lynn in the east.

The company's owners feel that the domestic solid fuels market may now have stabilized, but there is a considerable amount of uncertainty about this. On the other hand, they think that there might be an opportunity to move into different markets that could be serviced from the same basic resources.

This is a change in the market with important implications for the people in the workteam – and for their supervisors. Think about the issues carefully, and then write down detailed notes which would enable you to answer the following questions:

1   What can UK Flowlight do to assess how the solid fuels market, and the company's position within it, are likely to change over the next ten years?

2   If the solid fuels market continues to shrink, and the firm can't find new markets, what does this imply for its future and that of its employees?

3   What assets does the firm have that might be put to other profitable uses?

4   Given these assets, and the expertise within the company, what other markets could it consider developing?

Portfolio of evidence AI.3, DI.1

3 Work-based assignment

60 mins

The time guide for this assignment gives you an approximate idea of how long it is likely to take you to write up your findings. You will find you need to spend some additional time gathering information, talking to colleagues, and thinking about the assignment.

Even if you don't deal with the customer face to face, you or other members of your team may have contact in writing or on the telephone. You almost certainly contribute to a product or a service which, ultimately, the customer uses.

Perhaps you feel that you don't have customers at all – especially if your job is providing information or services to other departments in the same organization. But in that case your customers are the colleagues that you serve: the people who use whatever you provide. Each customer contact is an opportunity to improve the relationship with that customer. Even a complaint, if dealt with correctly and promptly, can improve customer relations.

What you have to do

1 Make a list of all your customer contacts, both internal and external, with a note of the product or service (information, for example) that you supply to them.

2 Choose **five** customers from your list and write down one way in which you could improve the service to that customer, so that he or she gets:

- the right product;
- at the right price (if any);
- at the right place;
- at the right time;
- in the right way.

Reflect and review

There are hundreds, if not thousands, of books, videos and training packages about marketing, but most of them deal with the technicalities of promotion, advertising, market research etc. Some, it is true, try to get to grips with the need to shape the product so as to meet the needs of the market. But few tackle the subject from the point of view of a non-specialist who wants to come to terms with 'the marketing approach'.

As you have seen throughout this workbook, marketing is not a cosmetic exercise – the 'icing on the cake'. It is about gearing the whole of the organization for market success, and everyone plays some kind of role in that.

Marketing is also about straight thinking. Ask yourself, 'What business are we in?' And the answer is only partly that you are in manufacturing, or retailing, or transport, or insurance, or local government or whatever. The most important answer is: 'We are first and foremost in the business of satsifying customers' needs.'

Your customers and their needs come first. They must determine what kind of product and service you offer and how you do so. If the product or service isn't right, then no amount of clever marketing will make it succeed.

The first workbook objective was:

■ When you have completed this workbook, you will be better able to understand the meaning and importance of the market and the marketing approach.

The startling success of Japanese industry in the last three decades has been put down to many factors. First they were said to be 'good at copying other people's products', but then it became clear that 'they' were also extremely good at innovation. It used to be claimed that Japanese people had 'little fingers, so they were good at assembling tricky things'. That was nonsense too, as was talk about 'oriental self-discipline'. The Japanese have proved as good at banking as at electronics.

The reasons for Japan's success are complex, but two stand out, and they are both to do with attitude and ways of thinking. The first is that modern Japanese industry and commerce had to be re-built from scratch after World War II. The old markets, relationships and structures were destroyed, and a lot of old ideas, attitudes and ways of doing things were swept away with them.

The second factor was the new ideas that were brought in. The new Japanese industries had to face a world market almost from day one. They therefore

73

had to adopt a 'marketing approach'. After the war, British car makers stolidly went on producing vehicles suitable for the winding roads and narrow streets of English counties, and they exported them on the assumption that they would do just as well in foreign markets. Their Japanese counterparts soon realized that foreign markets were different. They went out to acquire experience, and they designed and produced cars for success in those markets. This approach has been further refined in *kaizen*, or 'continuous improvement', which consciously sets out to maintain and improve competitiveness year on year.

■ What would moving towards a marketing approach mean for you and your team? How can you explain this approach to them and motivate them to accept the changes in thinking and behaviour that may be needed?

_____

_____

_____

_____

The second objective was:

■ When you have completed this workbook you will be better able to understand the marketing mix, and how an organization's resources are used to satisfy customers' needs.

The marketing mix means everything that the organization offers to its market. It starts with research and includes the product, the price, the service, the promotional and selling effort and so on. In a highly competitive world, any shortcoming in the marketing mix offers an opportunity for a competitor to gain an advantage. Everyone on the payroll contributes to the marketing mix in some way, and everyone therefore shares responsibility for helping the organization's marketing effort.

The idea of a marketing mix makes most sense when you compare it with what the competition is offering. What are they doing – or doing better – that you are not? If the customers see the competition as more exciting, professional, approachable, supportive, reliable and as a better bargain, something in your own organization's marketing mix needs to be changed. The marketing mix is also the source of those differences – let's call them advantages – that the salespeople need in order to make a case for customers to choose you rather than the opposition.

■ You will have been thinking about how to do better than the competition. Where are the main competitive strengths and weaknesses in your organization's marketing mix? What can you and your team do to build on the strengths and repair the weaknesses?

_____

_____

_____

_____

74

Having worked through the four sessions of this workbook, you may already be applying the ideas we have discussed both personally and with your workteam. Once you start thinking in terms of the marketing approach, you will find many opportunities to make a positive contribution to the organization's success in the market.

The final workbook objective sums up the overall theme:

■ When you have completed this workbook you will be better able to adopt the marketing approach and apply it to your everyday activities.

■ What are you now doing that is different from before?

_____

_____

_____

_____

■ What more will you do in the future to apply the marketing approach?

_____

_____

_____

_____

2 Action plan

Use this plan to further develop for yourself a course of action you want to take. Make a note in the left-hand column of the issues or problems you want to tackle, and then decide what you intend to do, and make a note in Column 2.

The resources you need might include time, materials, information or money. You may need to negotiate for some of them, but they could be something easily acquired, like half an hour of somebody's time, or a chapter of a book. Put whatever you need in Column 3. No plan means anything without a timescale, so put a realistic target completion date in Column 4.

Finally, describe the outcome you want to achieve as a result of this plan, whether it is for your own benefit or advancement, or a more efficient way of doing things.

Desired outcomes					Actual outcomes
1 Issues	2 Action	3 Resources	4 Target completion		

3 Extensions

Extension 1

Book   *Marketing*
Author   D. Mercer
Edition 2nd, 1995
Publisher Blackwell

Literally thousands of books about marketing have been written over the years, and hundreds are in print today. Some are specialized – dealing with marketing for small businesses, marketing services, international marketing etc. This one is a good general approach with plenty of useful examples.

Extension 2

Book   *Do Your Own Market Research*
Authors P.N. Hague and P. Jackson
Edition 1st, 1994
Publisher Kogan Page

There are, of course, practical limits on what an individual can do in terms of market research, and books of this type are mainly intended for people running their own small businesses. Even so, there are plenty of practical suggestions here that someone working for a larger company could adopt to find out more about their customers.

Extension 3

Book   *Sales Promotion Handbook*
Author   C. Brown
Edition 1993
Publisher Kogan Page

I recommend that you take up as many of the extensions as you can. They will further increase your understanding and interest, and the extra time and effort will prove very worthwhile.

These Extensions can be taken up via your NEBS Management Centre. They will either have them or will arrange that you have access to them. However, it may be more convenient to check out the materials with your personnel or training people at work – they may well give you access. There are other good reasons for approaching your own people; for example, they will become aware of your interest and you can involve them in your development.

4 Answers to self-assessment questions

Self-assessment 1 on page 17

1 These statements should read as follows:

a The market forces traders to face **competition** and presents customers with **choice**.
b The market is the net result of millions of individual **purchasing decisions**.
c The term **product** refers to whatever an organization offers to the market.
d Even the most successful product has a limited **life-cycle** [or **life-time**].
e Market research is about gaining greater **knowledge** and **understanding** of the market.

2 The marketing approach can be seen as providing:

a the right **product**;
b at the right **price**;
c at the right **place**;
d at the right **time**;
e in the right **way**.

3 The three important aspects of the marketing approach jumbled up in these letters are:

■ **advertising**;
■ **sales promotion**;
■ **selling**.

Self-assessment 2 on page 29

1 The marketing mix is the sum total of all the elements that make up the 'offer' that an organization makes to its market.

2 The most important factors in the marketing mix are usually:

■ the product itself;
■ the price;
■ the promotional and selling activities;
■ availability;
■ service.

However, there are many other factors, any of which may play a more important part in a particular case.

3 The three 'behind-the-scenes factors' that most affect long-term customer loyalty are:

■ the speed with which problems and complaints are tackled;
■ the attitude of the staff;
■ the general efficiency of the organization.

Self-assessment 3 on page 48

1 Among the external factors that can reduce competitiveness are:

   a **changed economic circumstances** (recession etc.);

   b **changed market conditions** (new competitors, new competing products).

2 The selling price of a product has to be low enough to **sell** [or **compete** etc.] but high enough to **make a profit**.

3 A segment of the market is a group of customers with distinct needs, quality requirements and spending patterns.

4 The cost-plus method of setting prices consists of working out the total cost of producing the product, and then adding a percentage for profit.

5 The main shortcoming of this method is that it does not take account of what the market is prepared to pay.

Self-assessment 4 on page 66

1 This statement is quite misleading. The ability to provide the product at the right place and time is a crucial part of the marketing mix.

2 The number of links in the chain can vary greatly. When a smallholder sells his or her own cheese and honey direct to consumers, no other links are needed. On the other hand, where a product is assembled in the Far East, sold wholesale to a trader in Italy and then distributed in batches to a variety of other traders throughout the EU, before filtering down to local retailers in the UK, the links may be many.

3 It is unfortunate if meeting the needs of the customer seems inconvenient, because a competitor will be prepared to do what the customer wants and thus gain the customer.

4 Time is very important – suppliers must be able to meet their agreed dates and times and, all other things being equal, the supplier who can provide the product soonest often wins the order.

5 The concept that 'time is money' is even more important than it has ever been, because of the much greater scale, speed and value of all commercial transactions.

6 Service organizations don't distribute in the way that manufacturers of physical products do; all the same, they have to make sure that their product is able to reach their customers (or perhaps vice versa). A college, for example, sells courses and skills. It may need to reach out beyond its local catchment by setting up 'satellite units' or offering courses by distance learning.

7 It is never wise to claim that one particular part of the marketing mix is all-important. It will vary according to the circumstances.

8 Customers are often prepared to be flexible when dealing with an established supplier, but no supplier should bank on this. In principle, the customer's needs should override those of the supplier.

9 While this is true, it doesn't mean that managers, supervisors and team leaders elsewhere in the organization can afford to ignore it.

10 I hope you agree with this statement: it is the main message of this workbook!

5 Answers to activities

Activity 38 on page 60

Anything which relates to Christmas, from puddings to wrapping paper, is subject to seasonal demand. Easter eggs and fireworks are examples of the same kind of thing. But jewellery is also very seasonal, for the same reasons as toys. And there are also definite seasonal peaks in demand for:

■ patio sets;
■ lawnmowers;
■ seeds and fertilizer;
■ caravans;
■ camping equipment;
■ sunglasses;
■ suntan lotion;
■ swimwear;
■ outdoor coats;
■ gloves;
■ bicycles;
■ antifreeze;
■ coal.

Activity 39 on page 63

■ Examples of Type 1 include many furniture stores, some shoe shops, and many hi-fi specialists.
■ Examples of Type 2 include department stores and firms such as Woolworths or Boots.
■ Examples of Type 3 include self-service stores, especially supermarkets.

6 Answers to the quick quiz

Answer 1   The market is the net result of the coming together of limitless numbers of buyers and sellers, and hence of millions of individual purchasing decisions.

Answer 2   Businesses need to keep bringing new products onto the market because all products have a limited life-cycle, and new products are needed to replace them.

Answer 3   Marketing is the process of identifying and satisfying the needs of the customer.

Answer 4   The marketing approach means gearing every aspect of an organization's activity towards satisfying the needs of the customer.

Answer 5   Market research is about gaining greater knowledge and understanding of the market. Market researchers try to find out about the present state of the market – who is selling what to whom, and for how much – and how this is likely to change in the future.

Answer 6   A product-led organization is one that develops products first and looks for markets afterwards.

Answer 7   The marketing mix is the sum total of all the things that an organization does that have some impact on customers' attitudes to its products – the total 'offer' that the organization makes to its market.

Answer 8   A premium product is one that can be sold at a higher price than competing products thanks to specially high quality, exclusivity or fashionability.

Answer 9   Many organizations try to offer a range of products because this enables them to reach a larger total market while using the same basic skills and resources.

Answer 10   Cost price is the basis of a selling price, but this can only be set after considering what competitors are offering, and what the market is prepared to pay.

Answer 11   The chain of production here will be a complicated one:

- raw material extracting and processing;
- manufacture and importation of components from several different locations;
- distribution, possibly through a number of different channels;
- retailing to the customer.

Answer 12   Non-commercial organizations should consider adopting a marketing approach because they, too, are providing products or services to their customers. They are increasingly subject to commercial pressures, and their customers are increasingly demanding to be treated as such.

Answer 13   If anything in the marketing mix isn't right, this will give competitors an advantage.

Answer 14   AIDA stands for Attention, Interest, Desire, Action – the process that advertisers and other communicators use to get results.

Answer 15   The missing element in this list is 'In the right way', meaning how the product is promoted and sold.

7 Certificate

Completion of this certificate by an authorized person shows that you have worked through all the parts of this workbook and satisfactorily completed the assessments. The certificate provides a record of what you have done that may be used for exemptions or as evidence of prior learning against other nationally certificated qualifications.

Pergamon Open Learning and NEBS Management are always keen to refine and improve their products. One of the key sources of information to help this process are people who have just used the product. If you have any information or views, good or bad, please pass these on.

NEBS
MANAGEMENT
DEVELOPMENT

SUPER **SERIES**

THIRD EDITION

Marketing and Selling

....

has satisfactorily completed this workbook

Name of signatory ....

Position ....

Signature ....

Date ....

Official stamp

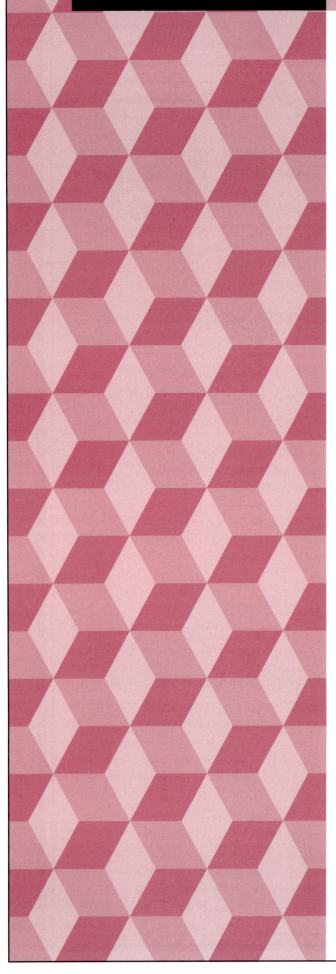

SUPER SERIES

SUPER SERIES 3
0-7506-3362-X   Full Set of Workbooks, User Guide and Support Guide

A. Managing Activities
0-7506-3295-X   1. Planning and Controlling Work
0-7506-3296-8   2. Understanding Quality
0-7506-3297-6   3. Achieving Quality
0-7506-3298-4   4. Caring for the Customer
0-7506-3299-2   5. Marketing and Selling
0-7506-3300-X   6. Managing a Safe Environment
0-7506-3301-8   7. Managing Lawfully - Health, Safety and Environment
0-7506-37064   8. Preventing Accidents
0-7506-3302-6   9. Leading Change
0-7506-4091-X   10. Auditing Quality

B. Managing Resources
0-7506-3303-4   1. Controlling Physical Resources
0-7506-3304-2   2. Improving Efficiency
0-7506-3305-0   3. Understanding Finance
0-7506-3306-9   4. Working with Budgets
0-7506-3307-7   5. Controlling Costs
0-7506-3308-5   6. Making a Financial Case
0-7506-4092-8   7. Managing Energy Efficiency

C. Managing People
0-7506-3309-3   1. How Organisations Work
0-7506-3310-7   2. Managing with Authority
0-7506-3311-5   3. Leading Your Team
0-7506-3312-3   4. Delegating Effectively
0-7506-3313-1   5. Working in Teams
0-7506-3314-X   6. Motivating People
0-7506-3315-8   7. Securing the Right People
0-7506-3316-6   8. Appraising Performance
0-7506-3317-4   9. Planning Training and Development
0-75063318-2   10. Delivering Training
0-7506-3320-4   11. Managing Lawfully - People and Employment
0-7506-3321-2   12. Commitment to Equality
0-7506-3322-0   13. Becoming More Effective
0-7506-3323-9   14. Managing Tough Times
0-7506-3324-7   15. Managing Time

D. Managing Information
0-7506-3325-5   1. Collecting Information
0-7506-3326-3   2. Storing and Retrieving Information
0-7506-3327-1   3. Information in Management
0-7506-3328-X   4. Communication in Management
0-7506-3329-8   5. Listening and Speaking
0-7506-3330-1   6. Communicating in Groups
0-7506-3331-X   7. Writing Effectively
0-7506-3332-8   8. Project and Report Writing
0-7506-3333-6   9. Making and Taking Decisions
0-7506-3334-4   10. Solving Problems

SUPER SERIES 3 USER GUIDE + SUPPORT GUIDE
0-7506-37056   1. User Guide
0-7506-37048   2. Support Guide

SUPER SERIES 3 CASSETTE TITLES
0-7506-3707-2   1. Complete Cassette Pack
0-7506-3711-0   2. Reaching Decisions
0-7506-3712-9   3. Making a Financial Case
0-7506-3710-2   4. Customers Count
0-7506-3709-9   5. Being the Best
0-7506-3708-0   6. Working Together

To Order - phone us direct for prices and availability details
(please quote ISBNs when ordering)
College orders: 01865 314333 • Account holders: 01865 314301
Individual purchases: 01865 314627 (please have credit card details ready)

We Need Your Views

We really need your views in order to make the Super Series 3 (SS3) an even better learning tool for you. Please take time out to complete and return this questionnaire to Trudi Righton, Pergamon Flexible Learning, Linacre House, Jordan Hill, Oxford, OX2 8DP.

Name :..

Address :..

....

Title of workbook :..

If applicable, please state which qualification you are studying for. If not, please describe what study you are undertaking, and with which organisation or college:

....

Please grade the following out of 10 (10 being extremely good, 0 being extremely poor):

Content   ....   Appropriateness to your position ....

Readability   ....   Qualification coverage   ....

What did you particularly like about this workbook?

....
....
....

Are there any features you disliked about this workbook? Please identify them.

....
....
....

Are there any errors we have missed? If so, please state page number: ....

How are you using the material? For example, as an open learning course, as a reference resource, as a training resource etc.

....

How did you hear about Super Series 3?:

Word of mouth: ☐   Through my tutor/trainer: ☐   Mailshot: ☐

Other (please give details):..

....

Many thanks for your help in returning this form.